D0817039

Financial Crises
in "Successful"
Emerging Economies

Financial Crises in "Successful" Emerging Economies

Ricardo Ffrench-Davis
editor

UNITED NATIONS
Economic Commission for Latin America
and the Caribbean

BROOKINGS INSTITUTION PRESS
Washington, D.C.

Financial Crises in "Successful" Emerging Economies may be ordered from:
BROOKINGS INSTITUTION PRESS, 1775 Massachusetts Avenue, N.W.,
Washington, D.C. 20036. Telephone: 800/275-1447 or 202/797-6258.
Fax: 202/797-6004. Internet: www.brookings.edu.

Library of Congress Cataloging-in-Publication data
Financial crises in "successful" emerging economies / Ricardo
Ffrench-Davis, editor.
  p.   cm.
Includes bibliographical references and index.
 ISBN 0-8157-0211-6 (pbk. : alk. paper)
  1. Latin America—Economic conditions. 2. Asia—Economic
conditions. 3. Financial crises—Latin America. 4. Financial crises—Asia.
I. Ffrench—Davis, Ricardo. II. United Nations. Economic Commission for
Latin America and the Caribbean.
  HC123 .F56 2001   2001003366
  332'.095—dc21

9 8 7 6 5 4 3 2 1

The paper used in this publication meets minimum requirements of the
American National Standard for Information Sciences—Permanence of Paper for
Printed Library Materials: ANSI Z39.48-1992.

Typeset in Adobe Garamond

Composition by Northeastern Graphic Services, Hackensack, New Jersey

Printed by R. R. Donnelley and Sons, Harrisonburg, Virginia

Contents

Preface

This book is the result of a project developed by the United Nations Economic Commission for Latin America and the Caribbean (ECLAC), with support from the Ford Foundation. The text encompasses five articles analyzing emerging economies that were generally rated as successful by international financial institutions and the financial press during episodes characterized by a broad supply of external funds. We include the cases of Chile, Korea, and Mexico in the critical years of the 1990s and Chile in the deep crisis of the 1970s. All of these economies were praised for their efficient public policies. They all experienced episodes of an abundant supply of financial capital, and they all suffered macroeconomic disequilibria as a result. We contrast these cases with the positive experiences of Chile during the Tequila crisis and of Taiwan during the Asian crisis.

Three of the articles are country studies, undertaken from a comparative perspective. The paper by Manuel Agosin, professor at the University of Chile, draws parallels between Korea and Taiwan. These two countries achieved a similar performance from the mid-1960s through the early 1990s, but their paths then diverged. The study analyzes the national policies adopted in each case and the underlying motives.

The article by Ricardo Ffrench-Davis and Heriberto Tapia, both economists at ECLAC, compares three positive financial shocks experienced in Chile: the liberalization of the capital account in the 1970s, which exploded in a massive crisis in 1982; a substantial policy shift in 1991–94 in the direction of a *prudential* macroeconomic management of the capital account, which kept Chile immune to the tequila crisis in 1995; and the capital surge of 1995–97, which culminated in a rather severe adjustment in 1999.

The third study is by Dr. Jaime Ros, Mexican economist and professor at Notre Dame University, who addresses the contrasting experiences of Mexico in 1991–94 and 1996–97. The paper examines the different domestic and external variables that explain the marked differences in the two episodes, and it evaluates the depth of the economic and social effects.

The fourth article, by Dr. Stephany Griffith-Jones of the University of Sussex, analyzes the current architecture of the international financial system and its incapacity for preventing crises or moderating the disequilibria that generally lead to crises. The article analyzes several recent proposals, including those of the author herself.

Finally, the paper by José Antonio Ocampo, Executive Secretary of ECLAC, and Ricardo Ffrench-Davis, which opens the book, examines why countries that were considered successful before the explosion of a crisis incurred a level of macroeconomic disequilibria that made them vulnerable to a financial run. We start by considering the nature of supply, focusing on investors who specialize in short-term, highly liquid operations. We then trace the evolution of the prices of financial assets, foreign exchange, and stock markets in the receiving countries, and we identify links with paths that culminate in unsustainable macroeconomic disequilibria. On the basis of this analysis, we expose five misconceptions that are commonly held among proponents of full liberalization of the capital account.

Heriberto Tapia provided highly professional support in preparing the final manuscript, verifying the technical content, and ensuring agreement between the Spanish and English versions. Lenka Arriagada was exceptionally efficient in assisting with the presentation of the final manuscript.

We thank ECLAC for providing a stimulating environment for policy-oriented research and the opportunity for independent analysis on a most relevant issue today. Our deepest thanks also go to the Ford Foundation for its support. Naturally, all the opinions presented here are the responsibility of the respective authors.

Financial Crises
in "Successful"
Emerging Economies

RICARDO FFRENCH-DAVIS
JOSÉ ANTONIO OCAMPO*

1 | The Globalization of Financial Volatility: Challenges for Emerging Economies

One of the outstanding features of modern financial crises is that they occurred in emerging economies that were generally viewed as very successful until the crises exploded. Moreover, recent crises have been radically different from those typical from the 1940s to the 1970s, which, in Latin America, displayed three major features that have been absent or relatively less important in recent experiences. First, past crises involved large fiscal deficits that were financed with external loans or, in the absence of such financing, by central banks. Second, domestic financial systems were repressed, a fact that was generally accompanied by private sector access to rediscount or bank loans at negative real interest rates. Finally, balance of payments crises were frequently associated with a sharp worsening in the terms of trade or explicit domestic policy decisions to overvalue exchange rates.

Over the past quarter century, a new variety of crises has gradually developed in Asia and Latin America. Four features differentiate them from the previous type. First, the international capital market has been the major source of shocks, whether positive or negative. Second, flows have largely originated from and been received by the private sector. Fiscal deficits, in contrast, have played a secondary role, and in most cases public finances have been sound. Third, these financial crises have mostly hit emerging

*We appreciate the assistance of Angela Parra and Heriberto Tapia.

economies that were considered to be highly credible and successful. In fact, the bulk of private flows has been concentrated on a small number of relatively affluent and well-organized developing nations. Fourth, these flows have been characterized by a lack of regulation, on both the supply and demand sides. Domestic financial systems have often been liberalized without the parallel development of a significant degree of domestic prudential regulation and supervision.

In practice, the differentiation between old- and new-style crises is naturally somewhat less clear-cut than the above description would suggest. An early example of the new variety was the Chilean experience of the 1970s and early 1980s, but the old type of crisis was still prevalent in the rest of Latin America during that period, with other Southern Cone countries in an intermediate position. In the 1990s, the new type generally predominated in both Latin America and Asia, but there were some mixed episodes in which features of both new and old crises were intermingled, with budget deficits and terms-of-trade fluctuations.

The evolution of private capital flows over the past three decades is well known. During the 1970s, a large supply of funds was made available to many developing nations. The 1980s brought a severe and widespread shortage of financing, particularly for the Latin American countries. In contrast, the Asian countries that were affected by the disturbances in the international financial markets adjusted rapidly (with the exception of the Philippines) and were able to leave the contagion effects behind. External financing returned to Latin America in the 1990s, but it was volatile. The resurgence of capital flows between 1991 and 1994 was followed by a sharp scarcity, especially in Mexico and Argentina, with a rather generalized portfolio outflow in late 1994 and early 1995. The so-called tequila crisis gave way to renewed access in 1996–97, but in 1998–2000 external financing was again in short supply as a result of contagion from the crisis detonated in Asia in 1997. Worsening terms of trade aggravated the recession. On all those occasions, changes in external financing were supply-led.[1] They had a strong impact on the national economies on both sides of the cycle, with contagion first of overoptimism and then of overpessimism.

Through 1996, the successful emerging economies of Asia appeared to be immune to the instability associated with capital surges, as illustrated by their performance during the tequila crisis. In reality, part of the outflows from Latin American countries were reallocated to Asia during that

---

1. Evidence shows that these changes have originated, to a large extent, in the sources of supply. See Calvo (1998); Culpeper (1995); Griffith-Jones (1998); Larraín (2000).

episode. The subsequent events show that immunity was no longer a feature of the East Asian economies, and the two regions now faced common destabilizing external forces.

The following section outlines the three capital surges experienced by Latin American countries since the 1970s. Subsequently, the paper reviews the main macroeconomic effects generated by capital surges and their policy implications. We then compare the specific experiences of the emerging economies covered by this research project: Korea and Mexico in the 1990s and Chile in the 1970s were all regarded as highly successful until the sudden outbreak of severe crises. The study contrasts these experiences with Chile in the early 1990s and Taiwan throughout the last decade, which provide examples of economies that deployed a set of prudential macroeconomic policies and thereby avoided domestic disequilibria and mitigated contagion. The paper then addresses five misconceptions that are currently in fashion. The final section summarizes some robust lessons for domestic policies and reform of the international financial architecture.

Three Financial Capital Surges to Emerging Economies since the 1970s

Purely financial factors have been changing in the world at a much faster pace than international trade and the globalization of production. During the 1970s and 1980s, many countries began to liberalize their financial sectors and to relax or eliminate foreign exchange regulations.[2] This contributed to a boom in international flows, which was facilitated by the revolutionary innovations in data management and telecommunications technology and the emergence of increasingly sophisticated financial techniques. The financial booms generally occurred within a framework of lax or nonexistent regulations and supervision, and most existing regulations were in fact procyclical.[3]

Net capital inflows to Latin America averaged nearly 5 percent of gross domestic product (GDP) in 1977–81, 1991–94, and 1996–97. Exchange rates appreciated in all three periods, which naturally led to a rapid increase of imports relative to exports, with the corresponding current account deficit being financed (indeed, overfinanced) by a sharp rise in the

---

2. Díaz-Alejandro (1985); Devlin (1989).
3. Ocampo (1999, 2001); Griffith-Jones (in this volume); United Nations (1999); Turner (2000).

stock of external liabilities.[4] All these macroeconomic variables experienced some overshooting.[5] Adjustment was frequently anchored to one dominant balance, which generated imbalances in other macroeconomic variables, as in a falling inflation rate associated with real exchange rate appreciation and climbing external deficits. Such adjustment was obviously facilitated by access to external financing, which most probably would have been absent in a dry foreign supply.

The increased supply of external funding in those three episodes generated a greater demand for such financing. Recipient countries that adopted procyclical or passive domestic policies experienced real exchange revaluation and large current account deficits. Because these were heavily financed by volatile flows of mostly short-term, liquid capital, the economies tended to become increasingly vulnerable to changes in the mood of external creditors; the outstanding case was Mexico in 1991–94 (see Ros, in this volume). Creditors with financial assets placed in the region became more sensitive to bad news as their exposure increased. The sensitivity rose steeply with the size of net short-term liabilities.[6]

The dramatic increase of international financial flows was more diversified in the 1990s than in the 1970s. The situation is potentially more unstable, however, inasmuch as the trend has shifted from long-term bank credit, which was the predominant source of financing in the 1970s, to portfolio flows; medium- and short-term bank financing; time deposits; and foreign direct investment (FDI; including acquisitions and other than greenfield investment). A very high share of the newer supply of financing is short term or liquid or both. The region thus saw a paradoxical *diversification toward volatility* in the 1990s. The relative improvement after the tequila crisis, with a rising share of FDI, still included a significant proportion of volatile flows.[7] The foundations of a broad liquid market for portfolio investment were laid down in the late 1980s through the Brady bonds and developed vigorously in the 1990s, with Latin America as a major destination for both bond and stock financing. This market offered the expectation of high rates of return during the upswings of the two cycles in the 1990s.

4. ECLAC (1995, 1998, 2000a).

5. When significant macroeconomic disequilibria persists despite repeated statements on the need to maintain equilibria, it reveals an inadequate understanding of how to achieve sustainable equilibria that are consistent with development. See Ffrench-Davis (2000, ch. 6).

6. Rodrik and Velasco (1999).

7. The positive link between FDI and productive investment is well documented (see Ffrench-Davis and Reisen, 1998, chap. 1). The link was weakened, however, by the fact that about 40 percent of FDI inflows in 1997–99 corresponded to acquisitions of Latin American firms rather than the creation of new capacity (ECLAC, 2000b, chap. 1).

In 1991 the stock of assets invested in Latin America by the new investors that had *discovered* the emerging markets was evidently below their desired stock level, but by 1994 it had become considerably larger. Net capital inflows were used to finance rising current account deficits, and external liabilities accumulated through time. This was sometimes accompanied by significant mismatches in the maturity structure of the balance sheets of domestic financial intermediaries, when short-term external funds were used to finance longer-term domestic credits. This issue was particularly severe in the dollarized segment of the domestic financial system and in those cases in which external interbank credit lines were used as a major source of domestic financing. Consequently, the region moved into a *vulnerability zone*, with the economy becoming increasingly sensitive to adverse political or economic news and "hostage to the whims and fancies of a few country analysts in London, Frankfurt and New York."[8] This situation was likely to "put the economy at the mercy of the capital markets' occasionally whimsical moods."[9] The longer and deeper the economy's incursion into that zone, the more severe was the *financierist trap* in which authorities could get caught, and the lower the probability of leaving it without undergoing a crisis.[10]

Mexico and Argentina were particularly vulnerable in 1994, while Chile had deliberately avoided venturing into the vulnerability zone. Meanwhile, East and Southeast Asian countries were just starting to take that risk in the first half of the 1990s, and the resulting mismatches in the maturity structure of the balance sheets of domestic financial intermediaries proved to be even more severe than a worsening net debt position. By the next cycle, several economies in both Asia and Latin America had penetrated deep into the vulnerability zone. Both regions suffered severe crises when the mood of the external market changed.

Worsening of Macroeconomic Fundamentals Led by Inflows

The economic activity of Latin American countries exhibited significant vulnerability to changes in international financial markets over the last three decades, which worked as an intensely procyclical factor for the

8. Rodrik (1998).
9. Calvo (1998).
10. The financierist trap refers to a macroeconomic policy approach that leads to an extreme predominance of or dependency on agents specializing in microfinance, positioned in the short-term and liquid segments of the market.

emerging economies. This vulnerability was associated with the volatility of international markets since the 1970s, as well as with the procyclical macroeconomic policies adopted by recipient countries. Several Asian emerging economies followed suit in the 1990s.

Annual GDP growth rose in Latin American countries from 1.3 percent in the 1980s to 4.1 percent between 1991 and 1994 and 4.5 percent in 1996 and 1997. Recessive adjustments took place in 1995 and 1998–99 (see table 1-1). Overall, GDP rose by a mere 3.3 percent in the decade (1991–2000). Given that GDP was highly unstable, however, the precise figure depends on the period chosen. For 1990–99 the growth rate was 2.8 percent, because the period starts and ends with a recession. From peak to peak (between 1989 and 2000), average growth was 2.9 percent.

A growth of productive capacity of around 3 percent (1.3 percent per capita) is remarkably low compared with the expectations generated by the structural reforms. Comparison with the previous golden age is striking. During the three decades from 1950 and 1980, GDP growth averaged 5.5 percent a year (2.7 percent per capita), with rather high domestic investment ratios sustaining these vigorous rates. In the 1980s, gross domestic investment dropped sharply, by 7 percentage points of GDP. The recovery in the 1990s was weak (see figure 1-1). In fact, investment grew much less during this decade than did capital inflows; a significant proportion of external flows thus financed increased consumption, crowding out domestic savings.[11]

Recovery from Recession

The domestic conjuncture has crucial implications for the link between capital flows and economic activity. When there is a binding external constraint, any inflow will contribute to relaxing it, thus facilitating a recovery of economic activity. Binding external constraints predominated during several episodes in many Latin American countries, and they were particularly widespread from the early 1980s up to 1990, in 1995 and in 1998–2000.

In the early 1990s, renewed capital inflows thus contributed to a recovery of economic activity, and they facilitated the adoption of successful anti-inflationary adjustments. Argentina and Peru, for example, both featured huge underutilization of capacity and hyperinflation; the disappear-

---

11. See Ffrench-Davis (2000, chap. 1 and 5); Uthoff and Titelman (1998).

Table 1-1. *Latin America and East Asia: Gross Domestic Product, 1971–2000*
Annual growth rate (percent)

Region and country	1971–80	1981–89	1990	1991–94	1995	1996–97	1998–99	1991–2000
Latin America								
(19 countries)[a]	5.6	1.3	-0.6	4.1	1.1	4.5	1.2	3.3
Argentina	2.8	-0.7	-2.0	8.0	-2.9	6.7	0.4	4.2
Brazil	8.6	2.3	-4.6	2.8	4.2	3.0	0.5	2.7
Chile	2.5	3.0	3.3	7.5	9.1	6.9	1.5	6.1
Colombia	5.4	3.7	4.3	4.3	5.2	2.8	-2.1	2.6
Mexico	6.7	1.5	5.1	3.5	-6.1	6.1	4.3	3.5
Peru	3.9	-0.7	-6.0	5.1	8.6	5.4	1.0	4.5
Venezuela	1.8	-1.5	5.5	3.2	-1.9	3.4	-3.6	2.1

	1971–80	1981–90	1991–92	1993–96	1997	1998	1999	1991–2000
East Asia								
(6 countries)[b]	8.1	7.0	7.3	7.3	4.8	-4.2	6.5	5.6
Indonesia	7.7	5.5	8.1	7.7	4.7	-13.2	0.2	4.2
Korea	9.0	8.8	7.3	7.3	5.0	-6.7	10.7	6.1
Malaysia	7.8	5.2	9.2	9.7	7.5	-7.5	5.4	7.1
Philippines	5.9	1.7	-0.1	4.2	5.2	-0.6	3.3	2.8
Taiwan	9.3	8.5	7.5	6.7	6.7	4.6	5.7	6.5
Thailand	7.9	7.9	8.3	8.0	-1.7	-10.2	4.2	4.5

Source: For Latin America, the United Nations Economic Commission for Latin America and the Caribbean (ECLAC). For East Asia, the International Monetary Fund (IMF), *International Financial Statistics*, November 2000; Asian Development Bank; J.P. Morgan.
a. National accounts expressed in U.S. dollars at 1980 prices for 1971–80, at 1990 prices for 1981–89, and at 1995 prices for 1990–2000.
b. In each period, each country's GDP was weighted by its average share in the regional output, expressed in current dollars.

Figure 1-1. *Latin America: Gross Fixed Investment, 1977–2000*

Percent of GDP

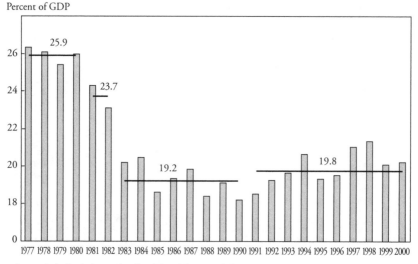

Source: Author's calculations, based on ECLAC figures, scaled to constant 1995 prices.

ance of the binding external constraint and the reintroduction of macroeconomic discipline to combat hyperinflation were strongly complementary. The monetary effects of reserve accumulation and the wealth effects of exchange rate appreciation tended to push up aggregate demand, which facilitated the recovery of economic activity. At the other end of the spectrum, capacity underutilization was not significant in Chile and Mexico. Consequently, the positive link between capital flows and GDP growth was not automatic, but rather was contingent on the capacity to transform additional external financing into increased productive investment.

On average, Latin American GDP rose faster in 1991–94 than the expansion of the production frontier thanks to increased capacity utilization. An estimated one-third of the 4.1 percent annual GDP growth in 1991–94 was based on this factor. In 1995, the binding external constraint again became a crucial variable, with GDP growth lagging behind capacity growth. Renewed capital inflows in the following years contributed to a recovery of economic activity, based to some extent on the excess capacity generated in 1995. However, the return of a binding external constraint in 1998–99, particularly in South America, led to a new recession.

One implication of this analysis is that any serious research should control for the huge swings in the rate of capacity utilization when measuring productivity and the performance of policies and reforms. In the

presence of excess capacity, recovery naturally yields high private and social returns, but they are built on preexisting disequilibria, that is, on for-
gone profits, wages, taxes, and employment that exist whenever the
economy is operating below its productive frontier or economically potential GDP. Whether economic recovery opens the way to more sustained
growth depends crucially on two dimensions. First, the speed at which capacity is expanded—through physical investment, investment in people,
and productivity gains—determines future potential growth. Second, the
sustainability of the macroeconomic environment that develops during
the recovery—namely, exchange and interest rates, current account deficit, domestic financial vulnerability, fiscal accounts, and asset prices—determines whether growth in aggregate demand can be sustained or
whether it will be subject to corrections associated with imbalances accumulated during recovery.

Overshooting in Emerging Asia and Latin America

The increased availability of financing in the 1990s removed the binding external constraint that had been responsible for the decade-long recession in Latin America. The bases for growth were not laid down,
however, as investment did not increase rapidly and macroeconomic imbalances built up. Effective output thus approached the production frontier, while exchange rate appreciation led to overvaluation.[12] Asset markets
also overshot, and a large stock of mostly liquid external liabilities accumulated (see figure 1-2). The region's economies therefore became more
vulnerable to future negative external shocks. With some variation, this
story applies to both 1991–94 and 1995–97, reproducing the path toward
the crisis of 1976–81.

In 1995, the tequila crisis had negligible effects on the Asian region,
even in economies with large current account deficits, such as Malaysia
and Thailand. Many outstanding researchers and observers therefore as-
serted in 1996 that such deficits were not relevant if investment ratios and
economic growth were high. Several Asian countries had successfully regulated capital inflows and foreign exchange markets for long periods.[13] Economic growth was actually sustained and extremely high. From 1970 to

12. Several Latin American countries implemented sharp import liberalization at the same time that
the exchange rate was appreciating. See Ffrench-Davis (2000, chap. 3) and ECLAC (1998, chap. 5;
for an English version, see ECLAC 1995). The average import tariff was cut from 45 percent in the
mid-1980s to 13 percent in the mid-1990s; nontariff restrictions were also reduced significantly.

13. On Malaysia, Indonesia, and Thailand, see Sachs, Tornell and Velasco (1996); on Korea and
Taiwan, see Agosin (in this volume).

Figure 1-2. *Latin America and East Asia: Current Account Balance,*
1990–2000[a]

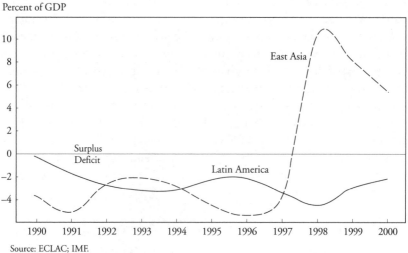

Percent of GDP

Source: ECLAC; IMF.
a. East Asia includes Indonesia, Korea, Malaysia, the Philippines, and Thailand. Latin America includes nineteen
countries.

1996, yearly GDP growth averaged 8 percent in Korea, Indonesia, Malaysia, Taiwan, and Thailand (see table 1-1 above). The investment ratio frequently exceeded 33 percent, with domestic savings ratios at a similar level.
Inflation was low (in the range of 5 percent a year), and fiscal budgets were
generally balanced or in surplus (with the exception of Taiwan). Meanwhile, average GDP growth in Latin America was 2 percent and the investment ratio fluctuated around 20 percent.

What is the explanation for the sudden worsening in Asia? First, export
performance in several Asian economies weakened. Export sectors that had
been experiencing notably dynamic demand suddenly faced tightening
markets, either as a result of a temporary excess supply or because specific
markets were reaching maturity.[14] The long Japanese crisis contributed to
the intensity of these problems.

Second, the global drive toward financial liberalization had also per-
meated several Asian economies in the 1990s.[15] China, India, and Taiwan
were three notable exceptions. Capital inflows and current account deficits
increased substantially in Korea and Thailand from 1993 on. External im-

14. Radelet and Sachs (1998).
15. Agosin (in this volume); Ariff and Ean (2000); Akyüz (1998); Furman and Stiglitz (1998); Jomo
(1998); Wang (2000).

balances were not associated with public deficits and did not imply losses of international reserves: in fact, in Korea, Indonesia, Malaysia, and Thailand, international reserves, fed by capital inflows, accumulated consistently between 1992 and early 1997, more than doubling in the period. All the data indicate that the cause of disequilibria was a rise in private expenditure led by capital inflows, which allowed liquidity constraints to be relaxed. The induced domestic lending boom was accompanied by bubbles in real estate and stock market prices. In some cases, real exchange rate appreciation and import liberalization led to cheaper imports, which further fed the import boom.

Third, most inflows were short term or liquid, including a large proportion of interbank lending.[16] Domestic balance sheets became quite vulnerable as a result of maturity and currency mismatches and the rapid rise of firms' leverage.[17] Weak prudential supervision of the financial system, which had not been a real threat in the previously repressed domestic markets, became evident with financial liberalization and the lending boom.

In these Asian economies, vulnerability was thus associated with worsening macroeconomic fundamentals led by a capital surge, which carried over to an exchange rate appreciation (moderate compared to that in Latin America), a boom in aggregate private demand (with a significant enlargement of the current account deficit by 5 percentage points of GDP in Korea, 2 points in Indonesia, and 3 points in Thailand), and an increased vulnerability of the balance sheets of domestic financial intermediaries. The disequilibrium was recognized by financial markets only in 1997 and resulted in a weighty bill in 1998. The policy failure was an error shared with the rather similar financial reforms conducted in Chile in the 1970s and in Mexico in the 1990s.[18]

Why the Market Fails to Avoid Overshooting

On the whole, the authorities took a procyclical approach in both Latin America and Asia, allowing capital surges to be transmitted domestically. They therefore fell into a *financierist trap*, from which it is extremely difficult to escape without a traumatic adjustment, involving outlier exchange or interest rates and considerable liquidity constraints that together generate a very unfriendly macroeconomic environment for firms and

16. IMF (1998); Radelet and Sachs (1998).
17. See Krugman (1999).
18. Ffrench-Davis and Tapia (in this volume); Ros (in this volume).

labor. Most authorities (as well as observers) took the view that nothing could or should be done during the expansive stages, or they preferred to benefit a little longer from the capital boom. The ex post consensus among observers, however, was that disequilibria had accumulated.

Given that voluntary flows cannot take place without the willing consent of both debtors and creditors, why did neither agent act in due time to curb the inflows well before a crisis? Some specialists recognized and warned of the growing vulnerability in all three episodes examined. Why, then, did the market fail to avoid major crises? [19] Asymmetries of information among creditors, lack of adequate internalization of the negative externalities that each agent generates (through growing vulnerability), and other imperfections of international capital underlie the cycles of abundance and shortage of external financing.[20] These factors contribute to herd behavior, cross-border contagion, and multiple equilibria.

Over and above these features, however, the particular nature of the agents acting on the creditor side is crucially important. Short-term horizons were a significant factor in the 1990s, as reflected in the volatility of flows that characterized the boom-bust cycles. The gradual spread of information on investment opportunities is another key influence. Investors from different segments of the financial market were steadily drawn into international markets as they took notice of the profitable opportunities offered by emerging economies. This explains why the three surges of flows to emerging economies were *processes* that went on for several years, rather than one-shot changes in supply.

On the domestic side, many Latin American economies were experiencing recession, depressed stock and real estate markets, high interest rates, and initially undervalued exchange rates; capital surges directed to these economies therefore could expect potentially high rates of return.[21] Indeed, in the early 1990s, prices of equity stocks and real estate were extremely depressed in Latin America. That allowed for a 300 percent average capital gain in the Latin American stock markets between late 1990 and September 1994, with rapidly rising price-to-earnings ratios (see table 1-2).[22] Average

19. For instance, see a warning advice on Latin America, as early as in mid-1992, reproduced in Ffrench-Davis (2000, chap. 9).

20. McKinnon (1991); Rodrik (1998); Stiglitz (2000); Wyplosz (1998).

21. A similar outcome tends to result in an emerging economy moving from a closed to an open capital account. The rate of return is naturally higher in the productive sectors of capital-scarce emerging economies than in mature markets that are capital rich.

22. Figures in current dollars; the real rate of return is obtained by adding distributed profits and subtracting dollar inflation.

Table 1-2. *Latin America and East Asia: Stock Exchange Prices, 1990–2000*ᵃ
Indexes (July 1997 = 100)

Region and country	Dec 1990	Sep 1992	Sep 1994	Mar 1995	July 1997	Aug 1998	Dec 1999	Nov 2000
Latin America								
(7 countries)	21.7	44.6	92.5	52.3	100.0	47.2	84.0	67.9
Argentina	13.4	46.9	78.2	53.5	100.0	53.4	86.7	64.6
Brazil	8.0	22.1	71.8	42.8	100.0	44.4	73.5	61.0
Chile	24.5	51.4	93.1	89.4	100.0	48.0	75.3	64.6
Colombia	16.6	65.0	113.1	96.3	100.0	49.9	44.9	26.0
Mexico	38.6	72.7	132.1	45.9	100.0	49.7	110.8	93.0
Peru	n.a.	n.a.	72.9	56.4	100.0	57.3	66.0	47.7
Venezuela	84.9	82.2	50.8	37.9	100.0	26.2	37.4	44.7
East Asia								
(6 countries)	n.a.	49.9	110.0	97.9	100.0	37.0	101.6	59.5
Indonesia	n.a.	53.7	84.2	71.6	100.0	11.1	37.0	15.8
Korea	n.a.	87.6	187.2	161.9	100.0	30.2	135.5	62.9
Malaysia	n.a.	63.7	119.0	103.5	100.0	16.8	49.9	42.1
Philippines	n.a.	67.1	134.6	108.6	100.0	30.4	61.0	32.9
Taiwan	n.a.	37.1	80.9	73.5	100.0	47.6	84.1	50.0
Thailand	n.a.	133.9	279.8	236.3	100.0	19.0	59.1	27.5

Source: Authors' calculations, based on data from the International Financial Corporation and Standard & Poor's, *Emerging Stock Market Review*, several issues.

a. The averages for Latin America and East Asia are weighted by amount of transactions. Values correspond to the end of each period, expressed in current dollars, excluding distributed earnings. Selected dates correspond to peaks and minimum levels for the Latin American average.

13

prices dropped sharply around the time of the tequila crisis, which produced contagion to all Latin American stock markets, and then nearly doubled between March 1995 and June 1997, pushed up directly by portfolio inflows.

Domestic interest rates tended to be high at the outset of surge episodes, reflecting the binding external constraint faced by most countries during periods of sharp reductions in capital inflows, the restrictive monetary policies then in place, and the short-term bias of the financial reforms implemented in Latin America.[23] Finally, the increased supply of external financing generated a process of exchange rate appreciation in most Latin American countries (see table 1-3). This encouraged additional inflows from dealers operating with maturity horizons within the expected appreciation of the domestic currency.

The interaction between the two sets of factors—the nature of investors and the adjustment process—explains the dynamics of capital flows over time. When creditors discover an emerging market, their initial exposure is nonexistent. They then generate a series of consecutive flows, which result in rapidly increasing stocks of financial assets in the emerging market. The creditor's sensitivity to negative news, at some point, is likely to suddenly increase remarkably with the stock of assets held in a country (or region) and with the debtor's degree of dependence on additional flows, which is associated with the magnitude of the current account deficit, the refinancing of maturing liabilities, and the amount of liquid liabilities likely to flow out of the country in the face of a crisis. The probability of a reversal of expectations about future trends therefore grows steeply after a significant increase in asset prices and exchange rates accompanied by rising stocks of external liabilities.

The accumulation of stocks and a subsequent reversal of flows can both be considered to be rational responses on the part of individual suppliers, given the short-term horizon of the principal agents on the supply side. Investors with short horizons are little concerned with whether capital surges improve or worsen long-term fundamentals while they continue to bring inflows. What is relevant to these investors is whether the crucial indicators from their point of view—exchange rates and real estate, bond, and stock prices—can continue providing them with profits in the near term and, obviously, that liquid markets allow them to quickly reverse decisions. They will continue pouring money in until expectations of an

23. See Ffrench-Davis (2000, chap. 2).

Table 1-3. *Latin America: Real Exchange Rate, 1987–2000*[a]

Indexes (1987–90 = 100)

Country	1987–90	1994:4	1995:1	1997:3	1999:1	2000:3
Argentina	100.0	63.1	63.8	65.6	56.6	56.9
Brazil	100.0	74.3	71.5	64.4	102.8	91.4
Chile	100.0	96.4	97.1	80.2	85.8	91.7
Colombia	100.0	80.4	79.7	71.2	80.3	97.4
Mexico	100.0	75.9	116.3	81.4	81.9	69.2
Peru	100.0	59.3	59.9	56.0	64.5	62.0
Weighted average (18 countries)	100.0	75.9	83.9	71.3	85.3	78.7

Source: Authors' calculations, based on official ECLAC figures.

a. Quarterly averages of real exchange rate indexes for each country with respect to the currencies of their main trading partners, weighted by the share of exports to those countries; inflated by external CPI and deflated by domestic CPI. For Brazil we weighted the Rio CPI index (two-thirds) and the new official series of inflation (one-third). Selected quarters correspond to peaks and minimum levels for the Latin American average.

imminent near reversal start to build. For the most influential financial operators, the more relevant variables are not related to long-term fundamentals at all, but rather to short-term profitability. This explains why they may suddenly display a radical change of opinion about the economic situation of a country whose fundamentals, other than liquidity in foreign currency, remain essentially unchanged during a shift from overoptimism to overpessimism.

The widespread belief that withholding of information prevented the Mexican crisis of 1994 being foreseen is therefore mistaken. While the provision of official information on international reserves was admittedly only sporadic, the key data—namely, real exchange rate appreciation, the high current account deficit and its financing with volatile resources, and low GDP growth despite booming flows—were available on a regular basis. Data were also available on the significant crowding out of domestic savings. However, Mexican policies were widely praised in 1993 by financial institutions, the media, and risk evaluators.[24] The incorporation of Mexico into the North American Free Trade Agreement (NAFTA) and the Organization for Economic Cooperation and Development (OECD) in 1994 served to intensify the trend. The crucial problem was that nei-

24. Gurría (1995, p. 281).

ther those on the supply side nor those on the demand side paid sufficient attention to the available information until after the crisis erupted.

It is no coincidence that in all three surges, loan spreads underwent a sustained fall while the stock of liabilities rose sharply, lasting for five to six years in the 1970s, for three to four years before the tequila crisis, and for over a couple of years after that crisis. This implies a downward sloping medium-run supply during the expansive phase of the cycle, which is a highly destabilizing feature indeed (see figure 1-3).

One particularly relevant issue is that firms specializing in microfinance, which may be highly efficient in their field but which are shortsighted by training and by reward, have come to play a determining role in generating macroeconomic conditions and policy design. This leads, unsurprisingly, to unsustainable macroeconomic imbalances, outlier macroeconomic prices, and an undermined environment for productive investment, particularly in tradables. Authorities should obviously be making decisions with a long-term view, yet they become seduced by the lobbying and policy recipes of microfinance experts and the financial press, which leads to irrational exuberance (to use Alan Greenspan's expression) despite evidence of inefficiency in resource allocation and total factor productivity. Macroeconomic authorities need to undertake the responsibility of giving priority to fundamentals in order to achieve macroeconomic balances that are both sustainable and functional for long-term growth. This requires that they avoid entering *vulnerability zones* during economic booms based on capital surges, since policy design is otherwise prone to being caught in the *financierist trap*.

The Economic and Social Costs of the Tequila and Asian Crises in Selected Countries

The economic literature commonly asserts that the only correct way to conduct policy is with an open capital account, as Mexico and Korea did in the 1990s. In reality, however, there is significant room for policy diversity. Chile and Taiwan provide two striking examples of policy diversity and successful prudential macroeconomic management of the capital account.

Mexico and the Tequila Crisis

The Mexican crisis that exploded in 1994 illustrates the harm that can be caused when the absorption of an excessive volume of capital inflows

Figure 1-3. *Latin America: International Bond Issues, 1992–2000*

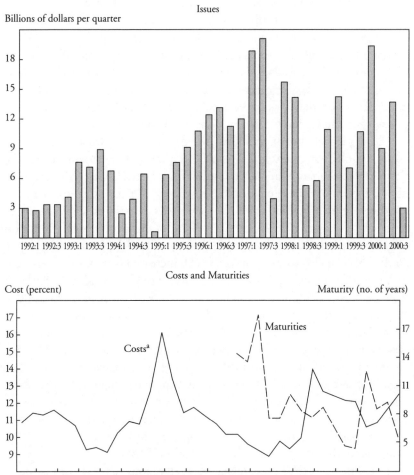

Issues

Billions of dollars per quarter

Costs and Maturities

Cost (percent)   Maturity (no. of years)

Source: ECLAC; World Bank; IMF.
a. Total annualized cost is equal to average differential on bond issues plus long-term U.S. Treasury bonds.

leads to the accumulation of a large stock of mostly short-term or liquid external liabilities and to a domestic credit boom.[25] Between 1990 and 1994, producers and consumers accommodated to a level of overall expenditure that rapidly outstripped potential GDP: expenditures exceeded effective

25. Ros (in this volume); Sachs, Tornell, and Velasco (1996).

GDP by 8 percent in 1992–94. The real exchange rate appreciated significantly, contributing to the sharp rise of the external deficit. Since the public sector was in balance, the disequilibrium was located in the private sector. When expectations of profitability were reversed, the amounts involved became unsustainable. Creditors cut financing sharply, forcing Mexico into a highly contractionary adjustment and a huge devaluation after the authorities adopted the flexible exchange rate. Despite the large package of international support that Mexico received in 1995,[26] GDP dropped that year by 6.1 percent and capital formation by nearly 30 percent.

GDP recovered strongly shortly thereafter, but the overall rise in GDP averaged only 3.5 percent in 1995–2000. The growth trend continued to be slow despite the fact that Mexico received a positive shock from the U.S. boom: export volume expanded vigorously by 17 percent a year in 1995–2000, four-fifths of which was directed to the U.S. markets. The investment ratio, which dropped sharply in 1995, did not fully recover until 1998. Real wages decreased substantially during the crisis and had not recovered by 2000. This was also true of poverty, which increased from 45 to 52 percent of the population between 1994 and 1996. Though the indicator fell back to 47 percent in 1998, it had still not returned to pre-crisis levels by 2000.[27]

The Mexican crisis did not trigger a widespread contagion effect throughout the region in 1995, in contrast to 1982. The most notable exception was Argentina, which experienced significant drops in GDP, employment, and investment in 1995. Nonetheless, many countries recorded negative flows in several segments of the supply of financing, particularly bonds, deposits, and flows to stock markets. Subsequently, the flow of funds became extremely abundant again. GDP recovery in Argentina and Mexico was particularly vigorous, since the sharp drop in both countries in 1995 had generated a large gap between effective GDP and productive capacity. This facilitated a significant degree of reactivation, which led to complacency—not only in those countries, but also in international financing institutions and elsewhere—regarding the effects of crises and the capacity to recover from them. However, as said above, growth in Mexico was slow for the six-year period 1995–2000 as a whole, and it was even slower in Argentina (1.7 percent), which entered into another severe recession in 1999–2000.

Significant differences also emerged between Argentina and Mexico. Mexico moved from a quasi-fixed nominal exchange rate to a flexible rate in

26. Lustig (1997).
27. ECLAC (2000c).

1995, which facilitated the adjustment to the financial shocks generated by the Asian crisis. Also, the country experienced a sizable positive shock associated with the rapid growth of the U.S. economy in 1998–2000. Argentina, meanwhile, was tied to the currency board; this limited the country's ability to confront the negative shocks from Asia, from the devaluation of the Brazilian currency, and from the revaluation of the dollar. Argentina's inability to facilitate the correction of relative prices through the active use of the nominal exchange rate was intensified by the strong international appreciation of the dollar and the persistent dryness in the supply of external funding. Indeed, the international capital markets underwent lengthy dry periods during the recent crisis, despite the boom in the U.S. economy and the acceleration in Europe in 2000. This indicates that financial markets may tend to recover slowly and incompletely, as was clearly the case in the 1980s.

Korea and the Asian Crisis

The East Asian countries suffered deep recessions in 1998, after decades of sustained annual GDP growth of around 8 percent. Indonesia exhibited a 13 percent recession, similar to the spectacular drop of Chilean GDP during the 1982 recession. Korea, Malaysia, and Thailand recorded reductions of 7 to 10 percent. The nature of the crises varied across countries in Asia. The Korean and Thai experiences, however, appeared to be associated with the capital surge of the 1990s and the resulting liquidity. During 1999–2000, Korea (and Malaysia) recovered faster than the other countries of the region. Notwithstanding Korea's impressive GDP growth in 1999 and 2000, the costs have been significant: in the period 1998–2000, GDP was about 12 percent below what it would have been had the historical trend continued, and investment fell by over one-fifth in 1998–99 as compared to 1993–96 (28.9 percent and 36.4 percent, respectively). Since the country also achieved an impressive external surplus of 9 percent of GDP in 1998–99, versus a deficit of almost 5 percent in 1996, disposable income was well below output.

The recessions in East Asia are comparable to those of Latin America in 1982–83, with drops in productive investment, banking crises, and social regression.[28] Apart from the intrinsic strengths of the Korean economic

---

28. For interpretations of the Asian crisis, see Krugman (1999); Akyüz (1998); Furman and Stiglitz (1998); Perry and Lederman (1998); Radelet and Sachs (1998); Reisen (1998); Stiglitz (1998); Wang (2000); Wyplosz (1998).

structure and of several other Asian economies (excluding Indonesia), four features of the international economic environment largely explain why the shift from recession to recovery came sooner in Asia than in the Latin American debt crisis: the plentiful supply of official external financing; rapid action spearheaded by the United States to refinance private credits, particularly interbank lending; significantly lower interest rates in the advanced economies; and higher growth rates, especially in the United States. The countercyclical policy implemented by the Korean public sector also played a significant role in the recovery; consequently, the fiscal balance swung from a surplus of 0.3 percent of GDP in the period 1993–96 to a deficit of 4.7 percent in 1998–99.

Until the early 1990s, Korea had extensive capital account regulations, based on a combination of market forces and state guidance.[29] In 1991, the country began implementing a broad range of measures aimed at liberalizing the capital account. Contrary to what is commonly assumed by observers, greenfield FDI—not acquisitions—was deregulated. Local firms and banks were allowed to issue securities abroad, and foreigners were authorized to purchase stocks in Korean companies subject to limits that were raised progressively starting in 1992. Foreign currency loans to local firms, trade credit, and short-term financing were also liberalized. Only long-term borrowing and acquisitions remained restricted. Under the new regulations, Korean banks and firms were permitted to engage in arbitrage between international lenders and local markets by borrowing short abroad and, in some cases, lending long at home. This practice would not have been allowed under the regulations prevailing before the liberalization drive in the early 1990s. In addition, Korea's sound creditworthiness afforded local firms lower spreads and more expeditious access to funding, which they used, in part, to borrow for financing investment and lending in other Asian markets.[30]

Capital inflows expanded hugely after liberalization and included purchases of stock shares, bond issues, and private loans to banks and nonfinancial firms. Liabilities became highly liquid, with short-term debt reaching twice the level of international reserves in 1996. This was not accompanied, however, by strengthened prudential regulation and supervision, in a replication of the negative Latin American experience.[31]

---

29. See Agosin (in this volume); Furman and Stiglitz (1998); Wang (2000).

30. In May 1995, one of the large international risk-rating agencies upgraded the sovereign credit rating of Korea (see Wang, 2000). In June 1997, the World Economic Forum classified Korea as the fifth most secure place to invest in the world (see Dean, 1998).

31. See ECLAC (1998, chap. 12). For an English version, see ECLAC (1995).

The process of liberalizing the capital account caused the exchange rate to appreciate with respect to the currencies in which borrowing took place, which encouraged further borrowing. Korea accommodated the capital surplus through import liberalization and currency appreciation, together with a relaxation of domestic liquidity constraints. The combined effect of increased imports and worsening export prices explain the rise in the current account deficit to 5 percent of GDP in 1996. Net inflows rose from U.S.$7 billion in 1992 to U.S.$24 billion in 1996, but gross inflows amounted to U.S.$49 billion.

The opening of the capital account represented a source of vulnerability, exacerbated by poor bank regulation and supervision. It left Korea prone to contagion, even though the fundamentals were generally sound. In fact, Agosin (in this volume) concludes that "the main factor behind the Korean debacle was the liberalization of the capital account, without the concurrent adoption of adequate bank regulation and prudential macroeconomic measures to discourage excessive capital inflow."

Chile and Taiwan: Going against the Fashion

Is it possible to forge ahead with policies that go against contemporary economic ideology? Two cases—Chile in the first half of the 1990s and Taiwan throughout the decade—provide evidence that it is indeed possible and can be an efficient and cheap way to avoid costly crises.

Chile deployed three types of capital account policy in the last quarter of a century.[32] The first was the plain neoliberal experiment of the 1970s, which culminated in a major crisis in 1982. That episode featured a drop in GDP of 14 percent, followed by an increase in open unemployment to 30 percent in 1983. The second approach was that taken from 1990 to 1995. In that period, authorities went against prevailing fashion by pursuing a set of active macroeconomic policies that included the prudential regulation of financial inflows. As a result, Chile was practically unaffected by contagion from the tequila crisis. The third type of policy, which was implemented after 1995, involved a relative relaxation of macroeconomic prudential policies. This gave way to a significant appreciation and allowed the external deficit to double from 2.5 percent of GDP in 1990–95 to 5.7 percent in 1996–97.

Chile's performance in 1995 was diametrically opposed to that of Mexico, despite numerous similarities in the two economies in the preced-

---

32. Ffrench-Davis and Tapia (in this volume).

ing years. The difference in results is attributable to the distinct divergence in macroeconomic policies in the first half of the 1990s. Toward the end of the 1980s, both countries had already liberalized their trade considerably, they had substantially improved their fiscal budgets, privatization was well underway, the annual rate of inflation was around 20–30 percent, and they showed similar domestic savings rates. In 1990–94, however, Chile and Mexico chose divergent approaches with respect to the management of capital inflows, exchange rate policy, and the prudential regulation and supervision of the domestic financial system. Chile's main advantage over Mexico in 1995 is that it responded to the abundance of external funds from 1990 to 1994 with a deliberate policy of active prudential macroeconomic regulation.

Instead of allowing in and spending all the available external supply, which would have led to significant appreciation of the peso and a rising current account deficit, the Chilean authorities chose to discourage short-term capital inflows. In 1991 a tax was imposed, and substantial non-interest-bearing reserves were required for external credit. The reserve requirement was subsequently extended to foreign currency deposits and investment in second-hand stocks, while primary issues of American depository receipts (ADRs) and FDI venture capital were kept exempted. FDI had to be held in Chile for at least one year. The financial system was subject to relatively strict prudential regulation, including a selective supervision of bank assets and required provisioning, as well as restrictions and drastic penalties on operations with related parties. This set of measures effectively discouraged speculative capital inflows.[33] Most empirical research shows that these regulations had a significant effect on the volume of short-term inflows, and, contrary to common belief, several studies also show an effect on total inflows.[34]

The smooth transition to democracy, an increasing international approval of Chilean economic policies, and high domestic interest rates combined to boost capital inflows to Chile after mid-1990; the process was earlier and relatively stronger than in other emerging economies. As a consequence of its prudential macroeconomic policies, however, Chile had only a moderate external deficit by late 1994, with high international reserves, a manageable short-term debt, a domestic savings rate that was ris-

33. Agosin and Ffrench-Davis (2001); Le Fort and Lehmann (2000).
34. See several references in the case of Chile in this volume. The classical paper arguing against the effectiveness of the Chilean reserve requirement is Valdés-Prieto and Soto (1998).

ing instead of falling (whereas the opposite was the case in Mexico), and a level of domestic investment that far exceeded historical records from 1993 onward. The exchange rate in 1990–94 was comparatively closer to equilibrium than in most Latin American countries, as reflected by a moderate current account deficit over that period.

Policy was effective in achieving its targets for most of the 1990s, but in 1996–97 the policy mix and the intensity with which it was applied remained unchanged despite a new vigorous capital surge to most countries in the region. Chile, in particular, was a target of these flows, since it had remained immune to the tequila contagion. This surge should have been met with increased restrictions on rising inflows. In the absence of such measures, inflows became excessive as investors were willing to pay the insufficiently restrictive cost of the reserve requirement, with no evidence of significant evasion; also, as Le Fort and Lehmann emphasize, some inflows that ought to have been made subject to regulation remained exempt.[35]

Although the Central Bank intervened heavily in foreign exchange markets, a sharp real exchange rate appreciation and a rise of the current account deficit were observed over the two-year period, which pushed Chile into a *vulnerability zone*. Nonetheless, the active regulation implemented up to the mid-1990s had left large international reserves, a low stock of foreign liabilities, and a small share of volatile flows. Unfortunately, those strengths were partially undermined by the excessive exchange rate appreciation and high current account deficit recorded in 1996–97, as well as the Central Bank's delay in reacting to the deterioration of the external environment. In particular, the Bank resisted market pressures for devaluation, concerned that exchange rate depreciation would increase inflation and worsen the balance sheets of the large domestic firms that became highly indebted in foreign currency liabilities in the period. The outcome was a sort of automatic adjustment featuring a sharp loss of reserves, a 10 percent fall in aggregate demand, a 1 percent drop in GDP, a 3.5 percentage point increase in the unemployment rate, and a marked drop in capital formation in 1999. Despite this recent recession, however, Chile achieved an average growth rate of over 6 percent for the 1990s, which was its best performance ever recorded in a decade.

The case of Taiwan is more straightforward. Taiwan similarly pursued a policy that went against the global trend, but its policy was notably tougher than Chile's. It kept in place a variety of direct capital controls that

35. Le Fort and Lehmann (2000).

had been initiated in previous years.[36] The Taiwanese dollar remained non-convertible. The authorities restricted inflows to banks, firms, and the stock market. Acquisitions remained forbidden (as they were in Korea until the crisis). Taiwan held quantitative restrictions on the stock shares that foreign persons and institutional investors could own. Domestic banks were also strictly supervised by the Central Bank. Consequently, external liabilities were low at the outbreak of the Asian crisis, because they had been restricted during the preceding boom in financing to emerging economies.

The Taiwanese economy exhibited a notably stable dynamism, similar to that experienced in Korea for three decades. Data on Taiwan are rather limited, but the available information is quite revealing. For the years immediately before the crisis (1993–96), the available information shows a GDP growth of 6.7 percent, with negligible capital inflows and a current account surplus. Taiwan was clearly outside the capital surge. Another remarkable feature of Taiwan is that its fiscal performance was notably different from that of most emerging economies: the government ran a significant budget deficit, with public investment financed in the domestic private market. In all, domestic private savings financed a fiscal deficit of 2.7 percent of GDP and an external surplus of 3.2 percent in 1992–96. The fiscal deficit coexisted with a stable real exchange rate and an inflation rate that was lower than in Chile, Korea, or Mexico.

Taiwan experienced some contagion and a few attacks on the Taiwanese dollar despite the palpably safe macroeconomic environment, which was further bolstered by huge international reserves (U.S.$88 billion in 1996). The attack quickly receded, however, and an initial devaluation of 20 percent quickly recovered by half. In 1998–2000 only a slight downward adjustment took place in economic growth, which fell to 5.9 percent (as compared to 4.2 percent in Korea). The strong adherence to real macroeconomic sustainability appears to have been extremely rewarding for Taiwan.

Misleading Recipes and Misconceptions in Fashion

A series of widely accepted hypothesis or beliefs form part of the conventional wisdom of the financial world, including international financial institutions, although these have undergone some positive changes in their

36. Agosin (in this volume).

perceptions in the wake of the Asian crisis. This section reviews five common assertions that we believe have significant policy and welfare implications. These beliefs are not validated by the actual performance of international financial markets and still less by the behavior of domestic markets in emerging economies.

Recovery from Recent Crises Has Been Rapid

A first, common assertion is that the recovery from crises has proved to be fast. This is fundamental for claims that authorities should allow the free, self-correcting operation of markets, since it is assumed that attempts to adopt policies to counter booms or accelerate recoveries tend to generate additional instability. Given that financial markets are the major source of economic instability for emerging economies, this line of reasoning implies that instability is inevitable but not excessively costly.

This assumption is inconsistent with the evidence. Crises generate medium- and long-term effects on financial markets. The most significant case in recent decades was the effect of the Latin American debt crisis on long-term syndicated bank loans, which were then the principal mechanism of financing. This form of lending disappeared after the crisis, and bank lending never returned to being a major source of financing for Latin American countries in the 1990s. Equally important, the Asian crisis had negative effects on bond financing, which have still not been surmounted. Issues have remained volatile, costs high, and average maturities low. The usual assertion that markets have recovered rapidly is based on a very partial view of external market conditions, which takes into account the ability of emerging economies to return to the market, but not the conditions of such access in terms of stability, costs, and maturity of financing.

As shown above, a rapid return to positive GDP growth rates is by no means a good basis for asserting that the effects of crises are short-lived. All countries that have undergone severe crises—including Korea, where recovery was very strong—display evidence that they were pushed into a lower GDP path. Three channels through which these medium-term or even permanent effects on GDP are transmitted are particularly important. First, investment falls sharply during a crisis, which affects the path of productive capacity. Second, the bankruptcy of firms generates a loss of capacity, as well as a permanent loss of the goodwill, productive and commercial networks, and social capital of those firms. Even firms that do not go bankrupt may pass through a long period of debt restructuring, in which prop-

erty rights are indeterminate; this uncertainty may affect their performance. Finally, domestic financial crises may ensue if the portfolios of domestic financial institutions deteriorate severely. The experience of
emerging economies (and Japan) indicates that restoring a healthy financial
system takes several years and generates adverse effects throughout the period in which it is rebuilt.

A growing body of evidence indicates that boom-bust cycles also have
ratchet effects on social variables.[37] The deterioration of the labor market
(through open unemployment, a worsening in the quality of jobs, or a fall
in real wages) is generally very rapid, whereas the recovery is painfully slow
and incomplete. This is reflected in the long-lasting worsening of Argen-
tine unemployment and Mexican real wages after the tequila crisis. It is
also reflected in Brazilian and Chilean joblessness following the 1999 recession, despite a fairly positive recovery in both cases.[38] The evidence on
poverty similarly indicates that a ratchet effect is present. As mentioned
above, poverty in Mexico had not abated to 1994 levels despite economic
recovery.

Opening the Capital Account Discourages Macroeconomic Disequilibria

It is commonly argued that fully opening the capital account deters
domestic macroeconomic mismanagement and encourages good macroeconomic fundamentals. This is partly true for domestic sources of instability, such as large fiscal deficits, permissive monetary policy, and arbitrary
exchange rate overvaluation. The volatility in market perceptions makes
this type of control highly unreliable, however: financial markets tend to
encourage lax demand policies and exchange rate overvaluation during
booms, whereas excessive punishment during crises may actually force
authorities to adopt overly contractionary policies (so-called irrational
overkill). Contrary to the usual argument, this is not associated with inappropriate information. Even well-informed market actors, such as credit
rating agencies or investment banks, usually operate procyclically.[39]

The opening of the capital account may actually lead emerging economies to import external financial instability, with capital inflows engender-

37. Lustig (2000); Rodrik (2001).
38. ECLAC (2000a).
39. On rating agencies, see Larraín, Reisen, and von Maltzan (2000). Market discipline can also
pose obstacles to necessary social reform (for instance, to higher taxes to finance efficient human capital investment) or to the ability to capture economic rents from natural resources.

ing a worsening in macroeconomic fundamentals. Thus while market discipline can serve as a check on domestic sources of instability—albeit not a very efficient one, given the whims of opinion and expectations characteristic of financial markets—it is a source of externally generated instability. Not only will the market inaccurately perceive some domestic policies as inadequate, it may actually induce key variables to deviate from sustainable levels. In other words, it is the market itself that generates incentives for emerging economies to enter a vulnerability zone during the booms.

Financial operators evidently fulfill a useful microeconomic function as intermediaries between savers and users of funds, as hedgers of risk, and as providers of liquidity. In practice, however, they have perhaps unwittingly come to play a role that has significant macroeconomic implications. Their herd-prone expectations have contributed to intensifying financial flows toward successful countries during capital surges, thus facilitating rapid increases in financial assets and real estate prices and sharp exchange rate appreciation in the recipient markets. Apart from the poor quality of prudential regulation and supervision in these markets, these macroeconomic signals contribute to prolonging a process that appears, misleadingly, to be efficient and sustainable (with good profits and loan guarantees, supported by high stock prices and the low value in domestic currency of dollar-denominated debt). In fact, bubbles are being generated with outlier macroeconomic prices, and sooner or later the bubbles tend to burst.

The general practice has been to encourage the recipient countries to accept the increasing supply of resources from the international financial institutions and financial specialists, and to praise them for doing so. The cost of external financing typically falls during boom periods, which implies that the market actually operates with a downward-sloping mid-run supply of funds. Excessive indebtedness and periods of massive outflows ensue, often prompting admonishment by the very agents who praised the economic performance of the emerging economies during the boom. There is an obvious contradiction between these two attitudes.

Fundamentals are clearly essential. There is wide misunderstanding, however, about what constitutes sound fundamentals. The inappropriate conventional definition, together with irrational exuberance, led to high positive grades being given to Chile just before the crisis of 1982, to Korea and Thailand in 1996, and to Mexico and Argentina in 1994. Something fundamental was thus missing in markets' evaluation of market fundamentals! The severe crises of these five countries cannot all be due to bad luck or contagion alone. Rather, certain crucial components of a comprehensive set of fundamentals deteriorated, led by massive capital inflows. A satisfactory definition of fundamentals should thus include not only low inflation, sound fiscal accounts, and dynamic exports, but also sustainable external deficit and net debt, low net liquid liabilities, non-outlier real exchange rate, and strong prudential regulation, supervision, and transparency of the financial system.

Corner Exchange Rate Regimes Are the Only Right Policy Alternatives Today

In today's open developing countries, the exchange rate regime is subject to two conflicting demands, which reflect the limited degrees of freedom that authorities face in a world of weaker policy instruments and reduced policy effectiveness. The first demand comes from trade: with the dismantling of traditional trade policies, the real exchange rate has become a key determinant of international competitiveness. The second is from the capital account. Boom-bust cycles in international financial markets generate a demand for flexible macroeconomic variables to absorb, in the short run, the positive and negative shocks generated during the cycles. Given the reduced effectiveness of traditional policy instruments, particularly monetary policy, the exchange rate can play an essential role in helping to absorb these shocks. This objective, which is associated with short-term macroeconomic management, is not easily reconcilable with the trade-related goals of exchange rate policy.

Many analysts call for limiting the alternatives to the two polar exchange rate regimes of a totally flexible exchange rate versus a currency board (or outright dollarization). The relevance of the dual demand is not captured in this approach, however, whereas intermediate regimes featuring managed exchange rate flexibility, such as crawling pegs and bands and dirty floats, attempt to reconcile these conflicting demands.[40]

Currency boards certainly introduce built-in institutional arrangements that provide for fiscal and monetary discipline, but they reduce or even eliminate any room for stabilizing monetary, credit, and fiscal policies, which are all necessary for preventing a crisis and facilitating recovery in a post-crisis environment. Currency boards thus allow the domestic transmission of shocks originating in international capital markets. In so doing, they generate strong swings in economic activity and asset prices, with the corresponding accumulation of domestic financial vulnerability.

---

40. See Frankel (1999) and Williamson (2000) on intermediate exchange rate policies.

At the other extreme, the volatility that is characteristic of freely float-ing exchange rate regimes is not a problem when market fluctuations are short-lived, but it becomes a major concern when there are longer waves, as has been typical of the access of emerging economies to capital markets in recent decades. In this case, volatility tends to generate perverse effects on resource allocation. Moreover, under freely floating regimes with open capital accounts, anticyclical monetary or credit policies exacerbate cycli-cal exchange rate fluctuations, with their associated allocative, wealth, and income effects. In fact, authorities have to adopt procyclical monetary and credit policies if they want to smooth out real exchange fluctuations under these conditions.

The ability of a flexible exchange rate regime to smooth out the effects of externally induced boom-bust cycles thus depends on the authorities' ca-pacity to effectively manage a countercyclical monetary and credit policy without enhancing procyclical exchange rate patterns. This is only possible under intermediate exchange rate regimes with capital account regulation. Because these intermediate regimes of managed flexibility grant a degree of effective, albeit limited, monetary autonomy, they provide the best oppor-tunity to respond to the dual demands on exchange rate policy. Such regimes obviously have shortcomings and may generate costs. First, all intermediate regimes are subject to speculative pressures if they do not gen-erate credibility in markets. The costs of defending the exchange rate under these conditions are very high; at critical conjunctures it may be advisable to move temporarily to full flexibility. Second, sterilized reserve accumula-tion during booms may also be costly. Finally, the capital account regula-tions that are necessary for managing intermediate regimes efficiently are only partially effective. All things considered, however, intermediate re-gimes offer a sound alternative to costly volatility.

External Savings Tend to Complement Domestic Savings

There is a strong correlation between investment and growth rates, with a significant interaction between capital accumulation and technical progress.[41] The Latin American experience in recent decades also provides compelling evidence that the way investment is financed is not irrelevant, because external savings are unstable and may crowd out domestic savings. Moreover, the induced real exchange rate effects of unsustainable external financing may lead to a misallocation of resources.

41. Schmidt-Hebbel, Servén, and Solimano (1996).

In the 1950s and 1960s capital flows to developing countries were mostly tied to particular investments and to public users, financing real assets mostly through direct investment and official project lending. The nature of financing tended to generate strong complementarities between external and domestic savings. Commercial bank lending in the 1970s and private portfolio investments in the 1990s, however, made the link between foreign savings and domestic investment weaker and less direct.[42] This disassociation between capital flows and actual investment has three implications: inflows may increase consumption rather than investment; inflows do not necessarily enhance the recipient country's ability to earn foreign exchange through expansion of capacity in the tradables sector; and foreign investment is easily reversed, insofar as the acquisition of securities is essentially a short-term commitment. The first of these effects is associated with the empirical fact that consumers and financial asset markets tend to respond more quickly to released liquidity constraints than do productive investors, who have a longer response lag because of the irreversibility and long maturity of their decisions. Nonetheless, construction generally responds faster than other forms of capital formation and is more prone to investment overshooting, given the effects of liquidity on asset prices.

The diverse behavior of markets and participants explains why the stability of flows has a significant effect on the relation between foreign and domestic savings. Uthoff and Titelman distinguished between the trend and deviations from the trend for foreign and domestic savings.[43] They find a strong crowding out of domestic by foreign savings when capital inflows are temporary (above or below the trend). Moreover, the effects of flows on the real exchange rate distort the allocation of investment. Real appreciation during booms may lead to a suboptimal allocation of funds to the expansion of productive capacity in tradables sectors (that is, it may generate so-called Dutch disease effects). This seriously weakens the mid-term objective of penetrating external markets with new exports and strengthens the negative vis-à-vis the positive effects of trade reform.[44]

Prudential Regulation and Supervision of Banks is Sufficient for Facing External Volatility

Lax or poor prudential regulation and supervision of domestic financial institutions obviously reinforces disequilibria. Strong regulation and

---

42. Turner (1996).
43. Uthoff and Titelman (1998).
44. ECLAC (1995, 1998, 2000b); Ffrench-Davis (2000, chap. 3); World Bank (1998).

supervision per se does not solve the problem, however. First, a significant share of capital inflows usually is not intermediated by domestic financial institutions; cases in point include Chile before the 1982 crisis and Korea and Mexico in the 1990s. Nonbank to nonbank flows have become increasingly important as a result of the type of diversification that has taken place in supply. Second, expectations are in themselves volatile. This applies not only to expectations of financial intermediaries, but also to those of national authorities and international financial institutions. Regulation and supervision may influence the transmission mechanism, but it can hardly affect the source of instability (volatility in expectations). Third, normal regulatory practices (including Basel Committee criteria) have procyclical features.[45] In particular, there is a lag between loan-loss provisions and overdue loans; and in turn, these lag behind the level of economic activity. Regulations are generally ineffective in dampening the strong incentive to lend during booms because overdue loans and provisions are low, prices and guarantees are biased upward, and high profit levels facilitate meeting the capital requirements necessary to increase lending. During crises, the level of overdue loans increases, and provisions must therefore be increased as well. This reduces the capacity to expand lending by biting into capital requirements, at the same time that low profits also reduce the funds available to increase the capital base of financial intermediaries.

Robust Policy Lessons

Several of the policy lessons that we developed in earlier works are reinforced by the research in this volume on the recent experiences in Asia and Latin America.[46] We group these lessons into five areas of action.

Maintain a Sustainable Volume, Composition, and Use of Capital Inflows

The volume of inflows must be consistent with the absorptive capacity of the host country. The failure to address this point is at the core of recent macroeconomic instability in emerging economies. Absorption capacity refers, of course, to both the use of existing productive capacity and the creation of new capacity. The composition of flows is relevant for three reasons. First, FDI (excluding acquisitions of existing assets) feeds di-

---

45. Griffith-Jones (in this volume); Ocampo (2001).
46. See also Ffrench-Davis (2000); Ocampo (1999).

rectly into capital formation, as do long-term loans to importers of capital goods. Second, volatile flows tend to have a direct impact on foreign exchange and stock markets and a relatively weak impact on capital formation, which requires long-term financing. Third, temporary capital surges tend to leak into consumption, since consumers can respond faster than firms undertaking irreversible productive investment.

Allowing an excessively large share of capital inflows to drain off into the stock exchange and the consumption of imported goods will usually create bubbles in asset markets and imbalances in the external sector, which tend to be unsustainable. Fast rising stocks of net liquid foreign liabilities, in particular, generate deep vulnerabilities. Consequently, higher ratios of long-term flows and productive investment imply a higher capacity for efficient absorption. This means not only that the economy will efficiently absorb a higher volume of capital flows, but that a higher flow will be sustainable.

Recent experience offers a dramatic demonstration that recipient emerging economies can pay a high cost for allowing the volume and composition of capital flows to be determined by the markets dominated by agents with short horizons. The microeconomic costs associated with the use of regulations on capital inflows should therefore be balanced against the social benefits in terms of macroeconomic stability, investment, and growth. Effective and efficient regulation can result in higher and sustained GDP growth, as occurred in Chile and Taiwan in the 1990s.

Avoid Outlier Prices and Ratios

Economic authorities must ensure that capital flows do not generate outlier prices or significant distortions of basic macroeconomic indicators, such as interest rates, exchange rates, aggregate demand, the composition of expenditure in terms of consumption and investment, and the production of tradables. An artificial increase in absorptive capacity characterized by outlier appreciation and reduced interest rates usually leads to costly adjustment. First, real appreciation during booms tends to distort the allocation of investment, seriously weakening the structural goal of increasing competitive export capacity. Second, if productive investment capacity reacts with a lag and domestic financial markets remain incomplete and poorly supervised, capital surges cannot be absorbed efficiently in the domestic economy and instead either leak to inefficient investment or crowd out domestic savings.

Capital surges should not be used to target a single domestic economic variable, such as inflation. This tends to throw other major variables off balance. It is risky to remain bound to a fixed nominal rate or to dollarize permanently, unless the economy shares an optimum currency area with the United States. As discussed above, intermediate exchange rate regimes, which cover a broad diversity, are generally preferable, as they are better adapted to managing the dual demands they face in emerging economies.

Adopt Flexible and Comprehensive Macroeconomic Regulation

Across-the-board opening-up of the capital account was premature. Countries should have postponed the process, proceeding selectively until other major reforms had been consolidated and new equilibrium prices established.[47] During structural adjustment, open capital accounts tend to allow capital flows to increase too fast, especially when international financing is abundant. This produces destabilizing macroeconomic and sectoral effects.

It is therefore unwise to make an inflexible commitment to fully opening the capital account, particularly in the light of the crucial importance of macroeconomic stability and the disproportionate volume of the international capital markets compared to the small size of emerging economies. As long as flows depend on short-term horizons and domestic securities markets remain shallow, this new modality of linkages with the global economy will carry the risk of severe instability. The recent experiences of Mexico, Korea, and Thailand attest to the wisdom of discouraging the accumulation of large short-term financial liabilities. Domestic prudential macroeconomic regulations offer the best defense given the present international financial architecture. If this approach makes use of a market-based set of policies, including, for instance, the Chilean-style reserve requirement, its level must be adjusted to the intensity of the supply of funds.

Sustaining economic growth in the face of volatile capital flows requires the deployment of a battery of policy instruments, including prudential price-based capital account regulations to deter speculative inflows and improve their maturity structure; an exchange rate regime based on a crawling band with intramarginal intervention or managed flexibility; the sterilization of the monetary effects of capital inflows; strong prudential

47. Williamson (1993).

regulation and supervision of the financial system, with countercyclical devices; and strong fiscal accounts, also with countercyclical mechanisms. Reserve requirements alone (or any other policy that increases the cost of external borrowing), while clearly useful, are insufficient for deterring speculative attacks when large exchange rate fluctuations are anticipated. Obviously, this implies that authorities must make an effort to avoid cumulative exchange rate disequilibria and sharp changes in the macroeconomic environment.

Reform the International Environment for a More Efficient and Balanced Globalization

The governance of domestic and international financial markets is key to the future of the world economy. A common factor in recent crises has been the great volatility of the most rapidly growing segment of international financial markets: namely, short-term and speculative funds. Successive waves of overexpansion, followed by financial panic, indicate that the market tends first to grow and then to contract more than is justified by economic fundamentals. These features are inconsistent with a balanced and efficient globalization. More energy is being spent on resolving crises than on avoiding them. While appropriate prudential regulation of domestic financial markets has obviously been lacking in most of the emerging economies affected by the crises, the lack of appropriate international and regional institutions to monitor such a sophisticated, but unstable, financial market is even more notorious.[48]

Focus on Crisis-Prevention Policy, Based on Prudential Management of Booms

The focus of attention for international and domestic institutions should be the management of booms, rather than the resolution of crises, which are usually the consequence of badly managed booms. Given that existing international institutions and instruments have been ineffective in warning of impending turbulence and instead have actually encouraged unsustainable booms, it is particularly relevant to design domestic prudential macroeconomic policies and appropriate domestic regulatory frameworks, aimed at controlling booms before they become unsustainable.

48. United Nations (1999); Griffith-Jones (in this volume); Ocampo (1999, 2001).

This principle also applies to the design of the international institutions required for a more balanced and stable globalization.

References

Agosin, M., and R. Ffrench-Davis. 2001. "Managing Capital Inflows in Chile." In *Short-Term Capital Flows and Economic Crises,* edited by S. Griffith-Jones, M. F. Montes, and A. Nasution. WIDER/Oxford University Press.

Akyüz, Y. 1998. "The East Asian Financial Crisis: Back to the Future." In *Tigers in Trouble: Financial Governance, Liberalisation and Crises in East Asia,* edited by K. S. Jomo. London: Zed Books.

Ariff, M., and O. G. Ean. 2000. "East Asian Response to the Instability of Financial Markets." In *The Management of Global Financial Markets,* edited by J. J. Teunissen. The Hague: Forum on Debt and Development (FONDAD).

Calvo, G. 1998. "Varieties of Capital-Market Crises." In *The Debt Burden and its Consequences for Monetary Policy,* edited by G. Calvo and M. King. Macmillan.

Culpeper, R. 1995. "Resurgence of Private Flows to Latin America: The Role of North American Investors." In *Coping with Capital Surges,* edited by R. Ffrench-Davis and S. Griffith-Jones. Lynne Rienner.

Dean, J. 1998. "Why Left-Wing Moralists and Right-Wing Academics Are Wrong about Asia." *Challenge* 41(2).

Devlin, R. 1989. *Debt and Crisis in Latin America: The Supply Side of the Story.* Princeton University Press.

Díaz-Alejandro, C. F. 1985. "Goodbye Financial Repression, Hello Financial Crash." *Journal of Development Economics* 19(1/2).

ECLAC (United Nations Economic Commission for Latin America and the Caribbean). 1995. *Latin America and the Caribbean: Policies to Improve Linkages with the Global Economy.* Santiago.

———. 1998. *América Latina y el Caribe: políticas para mejorar la inserción en la economía mundial,* 2d ed. Santiago: Fondo de Cultura Económica and ECLAC.

———. 2000a. *Economic Survey of Latin America and the Caribbean, 1999–2000.* Santiago.

———. 2000b. *Growth, Equity and Citizenship.* Santiago.

———. 2000c. *Social Panorama of Latin America, 1999–2000.* Santiago.

Ffrench-Davis, R. 2000. *Reforming the Reforms in Latin America: Macroeconomics, Trade, Finance.* St Martin's Press and Palgrave.

Ffrench-Davis, R., and H. Reisen, eds. 1998. *Capital Flows and Investment Performance: Lessons from Latin America.* Paris: Organization for Economic Cooperation and Development (OECD), Development Center.

Frankel, J. A. 1999. "No Single Currency Regime Is Right for All Countries or at All Times." Working Paper 7338. Cambridge, Mass.: National Bureau of Economic Research.

Furman, J., and J. Stiglitz. 1998. "Economic Crises: Evidence and Insights from East Asia." *BPEA 2:1998.*

Griffith-Jones, S. 1998. *Global Capital Flows.* Macmillan.

Gurría, J. A. 1995. "Capital Flows: The Mexican Case." In *Coping with Capital Surges,* edited by R. Ffrench-Davis and S. Griffith-Jones. Lynne Rienner.

Jomo, K. S., ed. 1998. *Tigers in Trouble: Financial Governance, Liberalisation and Crises in East Asia.* London: Zed Books.

IMF (International Monetary Fund). 1998. *World Economic Outlook.* Washington.

Krugman, P. 1999. "Balance Sheets, the Transfer Problem, and Financial Crises." In *International Finance and Financial Crises,* edited by P. Izard, A. Razin, and A. Rose. Dordrecht: Kluwer.

Larraín, F., ed. 2000. *Capital Flows, Capital Controls and Currency Crises.* University of Michigan Press.

Larraín, G., H. Reisen, and J. von Maltzan. 2000. "Emerging Market Risk and Sovereign Credit Ratings." In *Pensions, Savings and Capital Flows,* edited by H. Reisen. Northampton, Mass.: Edward Elgar.

Le Fort, G., and S. Lehmann. 2000. "El encaje, los flujos de capitales y el gasto: una evaluación empírica." Working Paper 64. Santiago: Central Bank of Chile.

Lustig, N. 1997. "The United States to the Rescue: Financial Assistance to Mexico in 1982 and 1995." *CEPAL Review* 61 (April). Santiago.

———. 2000. "Crises and the Poor: Socially Responsible Macroeconomics." *Economía* 1(1).

McKinnon, R. 1991. *The Order of Economic Liberalization: Financial Control in the Transition to a Market Economy.* Johns Hopkins University Press.

Ocampo, J. A. 1999. "International Financial Reform: The Broad Agenda." *CEPAL Review* 69. Santiago.

———. 2001. "Reforming the International Financial Architecture: Consensus and Divergence." In *New Roles and Functions of the UN and the Bretton Woods Institutions,* edited by D. Nayyar. WIDER/Oxford University Press (forthcoming).

Perry, G., and D. Lederman. 1998. "Financial Vulnerability, Spillover Effects and Contagion: Lessons from the Asian Crises for Latin America." *World Bank Latin American and Caribbean Studies Viewpoints.* Washington.

Radelet, S., and J. Sachs. 1998. "The East Asian Financial Crisis: Diagnosis, Remedies, Prospects." *BPEA 1:1998.*

Reisen, H. 1998. "Domestic Causes of Currency Crises: Policy Lessons for Crisis Avoidance." *Technical Paper* 136. Paris: Organization for Economic Cooperation and Development (OECD), Development Center.

Rodrik, D. 1998. "Who Needs Capital Account Convertibility?" In *Should the IMF Pursue Capital Account Convertibility?,* edited by P. Kenen. *Princeton Essays in International Finance* 207. Princeton University, International Economics Section.

———. 2001. "Why Is There So Much Economic Insecurity in Latin America?" *CEPAL Review* 73 (April). Santiago.

Rodrik, D., and A. Velasco. 1999. "Short-Term Capital Flows." Working Paper 7364. Cambridge, Mass.: National Bureau of Economic Research.

Sachs, J., A. Tornell, and A. Velasco. 1996. "Financial Crises in Emerging Markets: The Lessons from 1995." *BPEA 1:1996.*

Schmidt-Hebbel, K., L. Servén, and A. Solimano. 1996. "Savings and Investment: Paradigms Puzzles, Policies." *World Bank Research Observer* 11(1).

Stiglitz, J. 1998. "The Role of the Financial System in Development." Paper prepared for the Fourth Annual Conference on Development in Latin America and the Caribbean, San Salvador. World Bank (June).

―――. 2000. "Capital Market Liberalization, Economic Growth and Instability." *World Development* 28(6).

Turner, P. 1996. "Comments on Reisen." In *Promoting Savings in Latin America,* edited by R. Hausmann and H. Reisen. Inter-American Development Bank (IDB) and Organization for Economic Cooperation and Development (OECD), Development Center.

―――. 2000. "Procyclicality of Regulatory Ratios?" In *Global Finance at Risk: The Case for International Regulation,* edited by J. Eatwell and L. Taylor. New York: New Press.

United Nations. 1999. *Towards a New International Financial Architecture. Report of the Task Force of the Executive Committee on Economic and Social Affairs.* Santiago: Economic Commission for Latin America and the Caribbean (ECLAC).

Uthoff, A., and D. Titelman. 1998. "The Relation between Foreign and National Savings under Financial Liberalization." In *Capital Flows and Investment Performance: Lessons from Latin America,* edited by R. Ffrench-Davis and H. Reisen. Paris: Organization for Economic Cooperation and Development (OECD), Development Center.

Valdés-Prieto, S., and M. Soto. 1998. "New Selective Capital Controls in Chile: Are They Effective?" *Empírica* 25(2).

Wang, Y. 2000. "Getting the Sequencing Right: Lessons from the Korean Experience with Capital Market Liberalization." Seoul: Korea Institute for Economic Policy.

Williamson, J. 1993. "A Cost-Benefit Analysis of Capital Account Liberalization." In *Financial Opening,* edited by H. Reisen and B. Fischer. Paris: Organization for Economic Cooperation and Development (OECD).

―――. 2000. "Exchange Rate Regimes for Emerging Markets: Reviving the Intermediate Option." *Policy Analyses in International Economics* 60. Washington: Institute for International Economics (IIE).

World Bank. 1998. *Global Economic Prospects and the Developing Countries,1998–99.*

Wyplosz, C. 1998. "International Financial Instability." In *The Policy Challenges of Global Financial Integration,* edited by J. J. Teunissen. The Hague: Forum on Debt and Development (FONDAD).

MANUEL R. AGOSIN*

2 | *Korea and Taiwan in the Financial Crisis*

K orea and Taiwan fared very differently in the international financial crisis that started in July 1997 with the crash of the Thai baht. While Taiwan came through the crisis relatively unscathed, Korea experienced a major economic downturn bordering on a depression, the country's first since entering a period of fast growth following the Korean War. Prior to the onset of the crisis, both of these economies were viewed by commentators, international financial institutions, and academics as among the most successful developing countries in the postwar era. The crisis in Korea was certainly unexpected, perhaps more so than in most other stricken East Asian countries. As late as June 1997, the World Economic Forum had classified Korea as the fifth most secure place to invest in the world.[1]

The similarities between Taiwan and Korea prior to Korea's descent into financial distress in November 1997 are striking. Both economies had managed to sustain per capita gross domestic product (GDP) growth rates of

*I wish to thank the many people in Korea and Taiwan who helped with research for the preparation of this paper, especially Inkyo Cheong, Yophy Huang, Shin-Yuan Lai, Kenneth Lin, Chao-Chen Mai, Jae-Joon Park, Yung Chul Park, Julius Caesar Parreñas, Shi Schive, James Tsuen-Hua Shih, Sangdal Shim, Lee-Rong Wang, Yunjong Wang, and Rong-I Wu. Thanks also to Ricardo Ffrench-Davis and Jaime Ros for extensive comments on earlier drafts.
1. Dean (1998).

around 7 percent a year for over three decades.[2] Both started out at similarly low levels of income per capita in the mid-1950s. Both based their almost miraculous growth rates on export-oriented industrialization and the creation of new comparative advantages. Saving rates were high in both economies and especially so in Korea, whose domestic saving-to-GDP ratio was above 30 percent. Neither country relied on foreign capital: both had repeatedly recorded current account surpluses or negligible deficits (in Korea, up to 1995). Furthermore, both countries had a track record of excellent macroeconomic management, emphasizing prudent monetary policies, stable real exchange rates, and low inflation rates. Until the early 1990s, both economies had extensive controls over the capital account.[3] In sum, both Korea and Taiwan had achieved strong, sustained economic growth through the harmonious blending of market forces and state guidance.

The two economies also demonstrate important differences, of course. While Korean policy favored the formation of large conglomerates (the *chaebol*), Taiwanese development relied on small- and medium-size companies. Korean investment rates were consistently higher than Taiwanese rates, but the growth of Korean output was concentrated in more capital-intensive sectors than Taiwan's.

What is surprising, then, is the sudden unraveling of the Korean miracle. Korea was devastated by the financial crisis that engulfed the economies of the clearly more troubled countries of Southeast Asia such as Indonesia, Malaysia, and Thailand. In Taiwan, in contrast, the main manifestations of the crisis were a marked slowdown in export volume growth, a mild deceleration of the country's fast growth rate, and a temporary depreciation of the real exchange rate of about 20 percent.

This paper tries to explain the disparity in economic performance since the onset of the financial crisis in mid-1997. It finds that the main factor behind the Korean debacle was the liberalization of the capital account, without the concurrent adoption of adequate bank regulation and prudential macroeconomic measures to discourage excessive capital inflow. In Taiwan, the currency is still nonconvertible, and the monetary authorities continue to impose a variety of capital controls, which were very successful in preventing a build-up of external debt or a large inflow of

---

2. See World Bank (1993).

3. There is extensive literature on the development of these economies and the causes of their success. The two classic texts are Amsden (1989) and Wade (1990).

portfolio capital. Other factors include major differences in the structure of the economy, industrial organization, and bank regulation.

Economic Performance up to 1997

From 1992 to 1997, both economies grew rapidly, Korea at an average annual rate of 6.6 percent and Taiwan at 6.8 percent. Both countries recorded investment rates in line with their historical performance. The growth rates of export volumes were considerably higher in Korea, but Taiwan's export growth figures were nonetheless quite respectable (see table 2-1).

These economies were also similar in other respects. Inflation was low in both countries. With regard to the public budget, Korea had a more favorable performance than Taiwan. Korea was able to maintain its public finances practically in balance, while Taiwan ran deficits. The red ink in Taiwan, however, was due exclusively to investment expenditures. Taiwan also consistently ran public surpluses in current expenditure and income. The deficit on the capital account was financed largely with recourse to domestic borrowing.

Where these economies differ is in the balance of payments (see table 2-2). Korea tended to run current account deficits in the 1990s until the onset of the crisis, while Taiwan had a current account surplus equivalent to a couple of points of GDP. Up to 1996, however, the Korean deficit was very moderate. In 1996, the worst year, the deficit was almost 5 percent of GDP, declining to less than 2 percent in 1997.

The behavior of the real exchange rate also differed (see table 2-3). Korea's real exchange rate appreciated consistently but moderately during the period 1993–96, owing to large capital inflows. In contrast, Taiwan's real exchange rate was fairly steady in this period.[4]

It would thus have been difficult to predict the depth of the crisis by looking only at real exchange rate appreciation or the cumulative current

4. The degree of real effective overvaluation in both Taiwan and Korea was much greater than suggested by the calculation in terms of the U.S. dollar. The 32 percent depreciation of the yen vis-à-vis the U.S. dollar between the second quarter of 1995 and the first quarter of 1997 spelled overvaluation for all the currencies in East Asia, which were either pegged or quasi-pegged to the U.S. dollar. Taiwan and Korea both employed a quasi-peg. Prior to the crisis, Korea operated a crawling band exchange rate regime whose reference currency was the U.S. dollar, whereas Taiwan allowed the N.T. dollar to fluctuate within a narrow band around a reference price for the U.S. dollar.

Table 2-1. *Korea and Taiwan: Indicators of Economic Performance,*
1992–99
Percent, except as indicated

Indicator	1992	1993	1994	1995	1996	1997	1998	1999
Growth rate of GDP								
Korea	5.4	5.5	8.3	8.9	6.7	5.0	−6.7	10.7
Taiwan	7.5	7.0	7.1	6.4	6.1	6.7	4.6	5.7
Gross fixed investment (% of GDP)								
Korea	37.0	36.2	36.0	36.7	36.8	35.1	29.8	28.0
Taiwan	24.1	25.2	24.6	24.9	22.5	22.8	23.5	22.9
Export volume growth								
Korea	8.3	6.7	14.9	23.9	19.8	24.9	16.9	9.2
Taiwan	5.3	7.2	5.5	12.8	7.1	8.7	2.4	9.6
Export price changes								
Korea	4.8	3.2	1.8	0.9	9.7	—	−16.9	−2.2
Taiwan	−5.4	5.2	0.6	6.9	1.7	2.1	5.6	1.1
Inflation (CPI)								
Korea	6.2	4.8	6.2	4.5	4.9	4.4	7.5	0.9
Taiwan	4.4	3.0	4.1	3.6	3.1	0.9	1.7	0.2
Fiscal surplus (% of GDP)								
Korea	−0.5	0.6	0.3	0.6	0.3	−1.5	−3.8	−4.6
Taiwan	−5.4	−3.9	−1.7	−1.1	−1.3	−1.6	0.1	−1.3

Source: For Korea: Asian Development Bank, *Asian Development Outlook,* various issues; International Monetary Fund (IMF), *International Financial Statistics,* Washington, various issues; Korea Development Institute, *Major Indicators of the Korean Economy,* Seoul, various issues; The European Union Chamber of Commerce in Korea, *EU Chamber Monthly Bulletin,* Seoul, various issues; Sangdal Shim, "Recent Trends and Macroeconomic Forecast for 1998/1999," Korea Development Institute, Seoul, 15 December 1998, unpublished. For Taiwan: Chung-Hua Institution for Economic Research, *Major Economic Indicators for Taiwan,* Taipei, February 1999; Asian Development Bank, *Asian Development Outlook,* various issues; Central Bank of Taiwan, *Balance of Payments Quarterly,* Taipei, various issues; Central Bank of Taiwan, *Financial Statistics Monthly,* Taipei, various issues; Council for Economic Planning and Development, *Taiwan Statistical Data Book 1997,* Taipei; Central Bank of Taiwan, "Domestic Key Economic and Financial Indicators," Taipei, 1 March 1999. Data for 1998 and 1999 for both economies were partly drawn from Pacific Economic Cooperation Council, *Pacific Economic Outlook, 2000–01,* Asia Pacific Press at the Australia National University, Canberra, 2000.

account deficit. However, Korea did experience large capital inflows over a short period of time (1993–96). Net capital inflows were consistently larger than the current account deficit during this period, and the Bank of Korea accumulated considerable reserves (see table 2-4). By 1997 there were signs of increasing financial fragility. Short-term debt was rising very

Table 2-2. *Korea and Taiwan: Current Account Balance, 1992–99*

Current account balance	1992	1993	1994	1995	1996	1997	1998	1999
Billions of dollars								
Korea	−3.9	1.0	−3.9	−8.5	−23.0	−8.2	40.4	24.5
Taiwan	8.6	7.0	6.5	5.5	10.0	7.1	3.4	5.9
Percent of GDP								
Korea	−1.3	0.3	−1.0	−1.7	−4.7	−1.7	12.7	6.0
Taiwan	4.0	3.1	2.7	2.1	3.9	2.4	1.3	2.0

Source: See table 2-1.

rapidly: at more than twice the value of reserves, it had reached a level that made the economy very vulnerable to a change in investor and creditor sentiment. As shown in table 2-5, up to 1996 the rise in the short-term debt-to-reserves ratio was due not to a fall in reserves, which doubled between 1992 and 1996, but rather to the much faster increase in debt. In the second half of 1997, as the economy began to look increasingly fragile, capital outflows led to rapidly falling reserves.[5]

The Impact of the Crisis on the Real Economy, 1997–98

Economic performance was very dissimilar in the aftermath of the crisis. In Korea, the withdrawal of external capital that began in October 1997 caused a contraction in GDP of 6.7 percent in 1998. Unemployment, which had typically held at about 2 percent of the labor force, jumped to 8.6 percent by February 1999 and remained at over 5 percent at the end of that year.[6] Although inflation was originally forecast to rise well above 10 percent, the slowdown in the economy kept the rate of increase in consumer prices at 7.5 percent in 1998. A sharp correction in the won (which had initially overshot in the direction of depreciation) intensified the effects of the slow economy, resulting in an inflation rate of just 0.9 percent in 1999, far below its historical average (see table 2-1).

5. The first signs of trouble in the real economy appeared in early 1997 with the bankruptcy of Hanbo Steel and Kia Motors. While growth was still fairly strong in 1997, it was due mostly to overexpansion of exports by *chaebol* attempting to beat back the increased competitiveness of Japanese firms, which had benefited from the sharp fall in the yen beginning in mid-1995.
6. PECC (2000, p. 31); see also Shim (1998).

Table 2-3. *Korea and Taiwan: Behavior of the Exchange Rate and Short-Term Interest Rates, 1992–99*

Indicator	1992	1993	1994	1995	1996	1997	1998	1999
Short-term interest rates (lending)								
Korea	10.0	8.6	8.5	9.0	8.8	11.8	15.3	9.4
Taiwan	8.3	8.2	7.9	7.9	7.7	7.6	8.0	n.a.
Nominal exchange rate[a] **(national currency per U.S. dollar)**								
Korea	781	803	803	771	804	952	1,401	1,189
Taiwan	25.2	26.4	26.5	26.5	27.5	28.7	33.5	32.3
Real exchange rate (1992 = 100)[b]								
Korea	100	100	95	90	92	104	139	118
Taiwan	100	103	101	101	104	109	120	n.a.

Source: See table 1.

a. Period average.

b. Nominal price for the U.S. dollar, deflated by consumer price index, multiplied by the U.S. producer price index.

Table 2-4. *Korea: Capital Inflow, Current Account Balance, and Change in Reserves, 1992–99*
Billions of U.S. dollars

Year	Capital inflow	Current account surplus	Change in reserves[a]	Errors and omissions
1992	6.4	−3.9	−3.7	1.1
1993	2.7	1.0	−3.0	−0.7
1994	10.7	−3.9	−4.6	−1.8
1995	17.3	−8.5	−7.0	−1.2
1996	23.9	−23.0	−1.4	1.1
1997	−9.2	−8.2	23.0	−5.0
1998	−8.3	40.4	−25.9	−6.2
1999	12.7	24.5	−33.3	−3.5

Source: International Monetary Fund (IMF), *International Financial Statistics*, Washington, several issues.
a. A negative sign indicates an increase.

The Korean government was unable to control the outflow of capital, and it called in the IMF in late November 1997. The IMF put together a package of financial resources consisting of U.S.$21 billion to be disbursed in eleven installments over a three-year period. In addition, it secured commitments totaling U.S.$36 billion from bilateral and multilateral sources.[7] Disbursements were subject to the usual IMF conditions of tight money and the achievement of a fiscal surplus, despite the facts that the fiscal deficit was small and the economy had entered a steep recession. Surprisingly, it also required the Korean authorities to introduce the following far-reaching structural reforms:

—The complete opening of the capital account of the balance of payments, including the elimination of any remaining limits on mergers and acquisitions (M&A);

—The transformation of labor markets in the direction of Western institutional arrangements by abolishing lifetime employment practices and obstacles to firing;

—The restructuring of the *chaebol* to promote better corporate governance, greater transparency, and an end to what was viewed as crony cap-

7. For an analysis of the IMF program, see Y. C. Park (1998); Feldstein (1998); Radelet and Sachs (1998); Wang and Zang (1999); Furman and Stiglitz (1998).

Table 2-5. *Korea and Taiwan: Indicators of Financial Fragility, 1992–98*
Billions of U.S. dollars, except as indicated

Indicator	1992	1993	1994	1995	1996	1997	1998
International reserves[a]							
Korea	17.2	20.4	25.8	32.8	34.2	20.5	52.1
Taiwan	82.3	83.6	92.5	90.3	88.0	83.5	90.3
Foreign debt[a]							
Korea	44.1	47.2	72.4	85.8	155.8	137.0	139.1
Taiwan	19.9	23.2	26.2	27.1	27.5	38.5	30.0
Short-term debt[a]							
Korea	11.9	12.2	31.6	46.6	66.6	53.8	28.1
Taiwan	17.3	19.4	20.0	19.5	18.8	22.2	19.4
Ratio of short-term debt to reserves (%)							
Korea	69.2	59.9	122.7	142.1	194.9	268.8	54.0
Taiwan	21.0	23.3	21.6	21.6	21.3	26.5	21.4

Source: For Korea, World Bank, *Global Development Finance*, Washington, 2000; for Taiwan, Asian Development Bank, *Asian Development Outlook*, various issues.

a. End of period.

italism (basically, opaque relations between different affiliates and between the conglomerates and the government); and

—The closure of troubled banks, the promotion of bank mergers, the opening of the banking sector to purchases by foreign entities, and an increase in capital requirements and bank reserves to reflect Basel Committee standards.

The IMF adjustment program was bound to make matters worse in the short term. Higher interest rates were not able to contain the run on the won, which traded as high as W 1,960 to the dollar in December 1997, up from about W 830 at the end of 1996. If investors perceive a sharp increase in interest rates as reducing the likelihood of loan repayment, the increase will not only fail to shore up the value of the currency but could wind up fuelling further depreciation.[8] The combination of high interest rates and sharp depreciation caused widespread bankruptcies, as firms were both highly leveraged and heavily indebted in foreign currency. Company bankruptcies had extremely adverse effects on banks, many of which had already been weakened by currency and maturity mismatches between assets (which were mostly domestic currency denominated and long term) and liabilities (which were mostly foreign currency denominated and short term). Many banks failed and had to be rescued or restructured by the Bank of Korea.

As shown in figure 2-1, the sharp rise in both interest rates and the nominal exchange rate eventually subsided as a result of the evolving recession. The Korean adjustment was so severe that the current account swung from a deficit of U.S.$8.2 billion in 1997 (less than 2 percent of GDP) to a surplus of U.S.$40 billion in 1998 (12.7 percent of GDP). This was achieved basically through a fall in import volumes, since export earnings were almost flat. The IMF itself recognized that it had erred in imposing sharp fiscal restraints, and it relaxed its fiscal targets at the beginning of 1998.

Several authors criticize the conditions related to structural reform that the IMF imposed in Korea. Radelet and Sachs rightly point out that it is difficult and counterproductive to initiate reforms in the midst of a crisis.[9] Whether the reforms are even necessary is debatable. I argue below that the liberalization of the capital account without taking any precaution for the potential adverse effects of capital surges was one of the causes of the Korean crisis. This implies that further liberalization is unnecessary and probably counterproductive. Other reforms were ill-timed. Requiring

---

8. See Furman and Stiglitz (1998) for a full development of this argument.
9. Radelet and Sachs (1998).

Figure 2-1. *Republic of Korea: Exchange Rate and Short-Term Interest Rates*, 1997–98

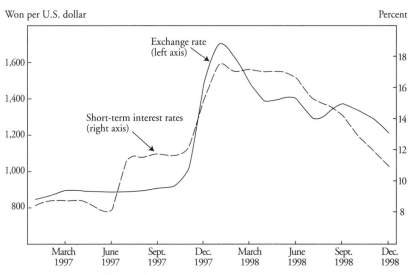

Won per U.S. dollar   Percent

Source: IMF, *International Financial Statistics.*

banks to increase their capital-asset and reserve-asset ratios during a banking crisis increased the intensity of the credit crunch and led to additional bankruptcies.

Feldstein argues that the IMF program for Korea constituted an unwarranted intrusion into issues that are far removed from the country's balance-of-payments crisis.[10] He holds that the changes sought in the IMF program, which should be left to national political processes and not imposed from outside under duress in times of crisis, were derived from long-standing demands on Korea to open its markets to Japanese goods and U.S. capital.

The impact of the crisis was much milder in Taiwan. There was a sharp deceleration in export growth and a modest decline in GDP growth, since domestic demand compensated the slack. As the crisis in Southeast Asia unfolded, the New Taiwan (N.T.) dollar came under strong attack. The initial response of the Central Bank was to defend the N.T. dollar and to accept a reduction in its comfortable level of foreign exchange reserves. When foreign reserves began to decline, however, it switched policies and stopped defending the currency in October 1997. The N.T. dollar quickly lost

10. Feldstein (1998).

Figure 2-2. *Taiwan: Exchange Rate and Interest Rates, 1997–98*

N.T. dollars per U.S. dollar   Percent

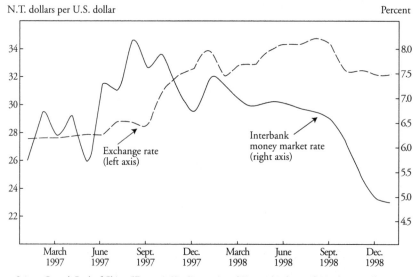

Source: Central, Bank of China, "Domestic Key Economic and Financial Indicators," March 1999; Chung-Hua Institution for Economic Research, "Major Economic Indicators for Taiwan," February 1999.

about 20 percent of its value in relation to the U.S. dollar (from N.T.$28 to N.T.$34 to the U.S. dollar). In late 1998, the N.T. dollar began to appreciate again.[11] At the same time, nominal interest rates began an upward trend in mid-1997 but fell again in the first quarter of 1998. By December 1998 they were lower than before the crisis broke (figure 2-2).

Thus the growth rate of the Taiwanese economy dropped temporarily by about 2 percentage points between 1997 and 1998, mainly as a result of the deceleration of export growth. Its unemployment rate remained largely unchanged at about 2.7 percent. Consumer price inflation continued to fall toward a zero rate. Taiwan was poised to resume rapid growth as demand for its exports recovered in 1999. In fact, Taiwanese firms may have strengthened their competitiveness by pursuing a policy of moving the export-oriented assembly of light manufactures offshore to locations in Southeast Asia, since the effects of the financial crisis have made those countries very attractive sites for export processing.[12]

11. In November 2000, the exchange rate stood at N.T.$31 to the U.S. dollar.
12. Huang (1998).

The Role of Economic Structure

Why Taiwan was able to stave off the crisis should be clear from the above analysis. What is much less obvious is why Korea was hit so badly. Korea was not a mismanaged economy, and it had high investment rates financed basically by domestic saving. A serious problem became apparent when the crisis broke, however. Korean firms had developed excess capacity, partly as a result of the depreciation of the yen beginning in the third quarter of 1995.[13] Rather than pulling back, Korean manufacturers responded with even larger increases in production and exports, which caused a sharp worsening of export prices in 1996.[14] This was particularly the case in the semiconductor industry, where the Korean response to gains in the competitiveness of Japanese firms contributed to the development of considerable excess capacity globally.

Government action to coordinate decisionmaking by individual firms had been on the wane for some time, as the government gradually handed over to the market most resource allocation decisions. Excess capacity problems had previously been dealt with through rationalization efforts led by planning agencies, but by the mid-1990s that restraint on the *chaebol* dominating Korean industry was simply no longer there.[15] These moves toward the liberalization of economic policy and the dismantling of planning instruments received impetus from international agreements on subjects such as export subsidies and financial services, under the aegis of the World Trade Organization (WTO). The *chaebol* were basically left to their own devices to pursue whatever course of action they perceived to be in their own interests.[16]

In Taiwan, increases in export volume were much more modest prior to the crisis, and average export prices continued to rise. Like Korea, Taiwan exports semiconductors, but firms were able to weather the global semiconductor slump of 1996 by reducing costs and switching their product mix away from those in excess supply. Strategic alliances between Taiwanese producers and leading firms in the United States, Japan, and Europe contributed to avoiding excess capacity.[17]

Another important characteristic of the *chaebol* is that they were

13. Of all the East Asian economies, Korea is the most competitive with the Japanese.
14. Y. C. Park (1998).
15. Chang (1998).
16. Y. C. Park (1998).
17. Yanagihara (1999).

highly leveraged. In 1996, the thirty largest *chaebol* had debt-equity ratios of 380 percent, compared to less than 100 percent for Taiwanese firms.[18] High leverage is good when the economy and profits are expanding briskly and when credits are renewed. In such situations, high leverage actually increases a firm's profitability, since interest rates are normally much lower than the rates of return on investment. What is a blessing in an expanding economy, however, becomes a curse in a shrinking one. When credits are not renewed or when interest rates rise sharply, companies go bankrupt more rapidly if they are highly leveraged than if their debt-capital ratios are more reasonable. Since Korean companies had never experienced a downdraft like the one that hit them in late 1997, their high debt-equity ratios seemed rational to them.

By contrast, Taiwanese companies are much smaller than their Korean counterparts, and they are consequently highly risk averse and extremely conservative in taking on debt. Investments are usually financed with retained profits and capital drawn from the extended family rather than from banks. This explains why the average debt-equity ratio in Taiwan is much lower than in Korea.

The Structure and Regulation of the Banking Industry

Many Korean conglomerates encompass a finance company, and they obtain funding from financial markets through these financial affiliates. Others have extensive dealings with a single bank, much in the manner of the relationship between the Japanese *keiretsu* and their main bank. In the years leading up to the crisis, the finance companies had been allowed to become full-fledged merchant banks, which improved the Korean conglomerates' access to international debt markets. Since merchant banks do not accept deposits from the public, it was generally believed that they did not need regulation. Commercial banks were, on paper, more tightly regulated. In practice, however, regulators turned a blind eye to many of their activities, in the mistaken belief that regulations were somehow contrary to the spirit of liberalization, particularly in view of the country's accession to the Organization for Economic Cooperation and Development (OECD).[19]

18. Y. C. Park (1998, p. 32).
19. J.-J. Park (1998) and personal communication.

Korean banks were accustomed to strong government guidance. Until the late 1980s, a large proportion of their assets was made up of so-called policy loans, which were loans made at preferential interest rates to firms in sectors that were favored by government policies for selective intervention. In the mid-1980s, however, the authorities began implementing a policy of broad liberalization of financial markets, and policy loans—which had represented 60 percent of bank lending in the late-1970s—were gradually phased out.[20]

Until the mid-1980s, then, commercial banks were either state-owned or under strong guidance by the planning authorities. Domestic banks were therefore unaccustomed to operating in a market environment, despite the recent liberalization. They had not yet developed expertise in credit analysis, risk management, or due diligence. Their ability to deal with the risks of foreign financial transactions was particularly inadequate.[21] Banking authorities performed poorly in the area of regulating and monitoring foreign financial activity. Prior to 1985, the economic authorities practiced extensive control over all items in the capital account, such that banking supervision and regulation in this area were redundant. This may explain why Korea had not developed a strong regulatory framework for financial institutions.

Taiwanese banks are very prudent in their lending policies, and they are also closely regulated by the Central Bank. Taiwanese banks were traditionally state-owned. The establishment of private banks was very gradual: even as late as 1990, twelve of the twenty-four banks in operation were state-owned. These banks accounted for 75 percent of all bank branches, 86 percent of all deposits, and 87 percent of all loans.[22] In 1991, rules governing the establishment of private banks were eased, and sixteen new private banks were opened. In addition, the Central Bank allowed the licensing of new foreign banks. Both public and private banks in Taiwan have long been subject to stringent prudential regulations.[23] In September 1998, for example, the capital adequacy ratio of Taiwanese banks was 11.4 percent—quite a bit above the Basel Committee norm of 8 percent. Taiwanese banks also face a number of restrictions on open

20. The liberalization of financial intermediation through formal banks caused the curb market to shrink considerably (Noland, 1996).

21. Y. C. Park (1998).

22. APEC (1998, chap. 9).

23. Yang (1998).

positions in foreign exchange, which must be approved by the Central Bank.[24]

These differences in banking structure and regulation show up in the behavior of nonperforming loans. At the outbreak of the crisis in 1997, nonperforming loans in Taiwan were only 4 percent of all loans, whereas they were 14 percent in Korea. This ratio inevitably increased in both countries as a consequence of the crisis, but in Taiwan they remained at a manageable level (5.5 percent in 2000). In Korea, in contrast, they came close to crippling the banking sector, peaking in 1998 at 25 percent of all loans (or 34 percent of GDP) and then gradually falling back to an estimated 18 percent in 2000.[25] This forced the Bank of Korea to intervene by liquidating banks, merging weak banks with stronger ones, injecting more capital into banks deemed to be salvageable, and selling others off to foreign banks. Nonperforming loans are still a major stumbling block in the ability of the banking sector to grant fresh credit to the private sector.

Policies on Capital Inflows

In globalized financial markets, it is difficult for a country to run into an international financial crisis without first having experienced large capital inflows. A country can have a balance-of-payments crisis simply because of bad domestic policies, of course, but the IMF is prepared to deal with this type of crisis by means of conditional lending. Another possible source of crisis in the absence of large capital inflows might be a currency crisis produced entirely by contagion. If a crisis elsewhere induces fears of a possible depreciation of the currency and if international financial transactions are reasonably free, then national and foreign financial investors could cause a crisis by selling the domestic currency and buying foreign exchange. Such contagion was a factor explaining why countries that had been quite well managed experienced difficult times during the recent crisis regardless of past policy. Examples include Chile and Hong Kong.[26] Despite the enormous differences between these two economies, they both were pursuing rather prudent policies before the financial crisis. Nonetheless, they both suffered significant contagion.

24. Personal communication with Central Bank officials.
25. Data on nonperforming loans are taken from Goldman Sachs, March 1998; J.P. Morgan, April 1998; *Asiaweek*, "The Asiaweek Financial 500," September 19, 1997, and September 11, 1998.
26. On Chile, see Ffrench-Davis and Tapia (in this volume).

However, the new breed of crisis associated with the globalization of finance is generally preceded by a strong upsurge in capital inflow. This was the case in Mexico prior to 1994.[27] It was universally the case in the countries that were most badly hit by the recent financial crisis: Brazil, Indonesia, Korea, Malaysia, Philippines, Russia, and Thailand. Large capital inflows can occur for a variety of reasons, including the perception by foreign financial investors that a country is doing things well or simply that its currency will appreciate because they believe others think it will.[28] Since interest rates are normally higher in emerging markets than in mature ones, expectations of currency appreciation can produce very large inflows.

Such inflows are often not marginal for an individual recipient. They can therefore have important negative externalities: they can generate current account deficits, appreciate the exchange rate, and unleash asset price bubbles. They also often increase the level of short-term debt relative to international reserves. At the same time, the short-term nature of the inflows makes it easy for investors to flee and for creditors to not renew their lending when they sense trouble.[29] Consequently, any worsening of fundamentals that generates perceptions of vulnerability will cause capital inflows to slow down, usually quite abruptly, and then to reverse direction. When the country has lost sufficient reserves, foreign and domestic financial investors discover exchange rate risk. As the fear of depreciation gathers momentum, everybody seeks to liquidate positions in domestic currency, accelerating the loss of reserves and precipitating a full-blown balance-of-payments crisis.

These stylized facts fit the case of Korea fairly well. Korean banks intermediated huge capital inflows and financial resources in the 1990s. Even so, the current account was not out of control despite being in deficit (it had been in surplus in the second half of the 1980s). Although the real exchange rate appreciated as a result of capital inflow, the degree of appreciation was not excessive by recent standards. Financial fragility rose to very dangerous levels, however: the ratio of short-term debt to international reserves exceeded 200 percent in 1997, making the economy very vulnerable to capital flight by scared investors and creditors (see table 2-5).

---

27. See Ros (in this volume).

28. This is a peculiar international version of Keynes's beauty contests (see Eatwell, 1997, p. 243). Some investors are more concerned with what other investors are doing than with the underlying worth of assets. When these participants predominate over the so-called fundamentalists, financial markets can be very volatile indeed.

29. Ffrench-Davis and Ocampo (in this volume).

Korea introduced a broad range of measures in 1991–93 to liberalize the capital account. In 1991, all remaining restrictions on greenfield foreign direct investment (FDI) were scrapped, and resident companies and banks were allowed to issue securities abroad. Beginning in January 1992, foreigners were allowed to purchase stocks in individual Korean companies, with the limitation that a maximum of 10 percent of a company's equity could be owned by foreigners as a group.[30] Both the aggregate and individual investors' ceilings were gradually enlarged thereafter.

Short-term flows, however, were liberalized ahead of most long-term flows. Ceilings on loans in foreign exchange to domestic firms were lifted in 1994, but ceilings on banks' long- and medium-term borrowing from international financial markets were not. Only trade credits and other short-term borrowing abroad were liberalized. This forced banks to raise short-term credit to finance long-term loans to the *chaebol*.[31] Other types of long-term capital movements were also excluded from the trend toward liberalizing the capital account. These included purchases of domestic bonds by foreigners, as well as a virtual ban on M&A owing to restrictions on foreign ownership of existing Korean companies. The crisis and the conditions attached to the IMF program eliminated most of the remaining restrictions. By the end of 1997, the aggregate ceiling for foreign portfolio investment had been raised to 55 percent of a company's equity. All restrictions on M&A were eliminated in May 1998.[32]

The short end of the financial market was thus opened up ahead of bond markets, long-term bank finance, and the market for corporate control. The authorities seemed to hold the erroneous view that short-term finance (most of which was assumed to be trade related) is self-liquidating and, as such, unlikely to generate overindebtedness. However, Korean banks and firms were borrowing large sums of short-term funds to finance long-term investments. Even when the authorities became aware of the deteriorating quality of bank assets and the increasing mismatches in the term structure of assets and liabilities, they failed to intervene, perhaps because they lacked experience and resources, but also, to a significant degree, because they were influenced by the atmosphere of euphoria predominating in international financial markets.[33]

30. Park (1996). Until that date, foreigners were allowed to invest in Korea's stock market only through authorized open-end mutual funds.
31. Y. C. Park (1998).
32. Wang and Zang (1999, chap. 9).
33. Y. C. Park (1998).

The flows that followed liberalization in the early to mid-1990s were enormous (see table 2-6). Curiously, the big increases were not in FDI (perhaps because of restrictions on M&A), but in portfolio transactions and bank lending. Purchases of shares on the Seoul market jumped from U.S.$2.5 billion in 1992 to U.S.$6.6 billion in 1993. Since Korean companies are among the world's most competitive, they were undoubtedly very attractive to foreign portfolio investors. Thus much of the equity portfolio inflows that took place after 1992 was a stock adjustment phenomenon that should have been fully anticipated by the authorities. Unfortunately, it was not. This lack of foresight fueled the capital surge.

Debt-creating portfolio inflows rose spectacularly, from U.S.$2.5 billion in 1992 to U.S.$15.2 billion in 1996. These were mostly securitized forms of bank lending. International banks were acting as middlemen in the placement of securities by Korean banks (and also by banks from other East Asian countries) in international financial markets.[34] Private credit to both banks and nonfinancial firms also rose dramatically. At the same time, Korea experienced large outflows in the form of debt-creating portfolio flows and lending by banks and nonbanks. This is an indication that Korean banks and firms were engaging in interest rate arbitrage between international capital markets, on the one hand, and Korean or other markets, on the other. As shown above in table 2-4, net capital inflows consistently exceeded the current account deficit plus reserve accumulation between 1993 and 1996. Large negative errors and omissions demonstrate that Korean banks and *chaebol* were engaging in financial investments in other countries, such as Indonesia and Thailand. There are even some reports that Korean banks were purchasing Russian government bonds.

Financial liberalization, then, led to large capital inflows and outflows. Korean banks borrowed short abroad in order to lend long to the *chaebol*, which borrowed to finance aggressive investment plans. In some instances, the borrowers on international markets were the *chaebol* themselves or their foreign subsidiaries. This mismatch between the maturity structure of assets and liabilities was accompanied by an equally dangerous currency mismatch: Korean banks took on debt in foreign exchange and lent in won (and also in baht, Indonesian rupiahs, and other currencies). Banks became totally illiquid during the crisis when foreign creditors refused to roll over short-term loans. The first to flee were the foreign equity investors,

---

34. For a description, see Kregel (1998a, 1998b); Taylor (1999).

Table 2-6. *Korea: Capital inflows, 1992–99*
Billions of U.S. dollars

Item	1992	1993	1994	1995	1996	1997	1998	1999[b]
Foreign direct investment								
Inflows	0.7	0.6	0.8	1.8	2.3	2.8	5.4	9.3
Outflows	-1.2	-1.3	-2.5	-3.5	-4.7	-4.4	-4.7	-4.2
Portfolio								
Inflows: equity	2.5	6.6	3.6	4.2	6.0	2.5	3.9	12.1
Inflows: debt	2.5	3.9	4.5	9.7	15.2	9.8	-4.1	-5.1
Outflows: equity	–	-0.2	-0.4	-0.2	-0.7	-0.3	0.0	-0.3
Outflows: debt	0.8	-0.3	-1.6	-2.0	-5.3	2.3	-1.6	2.0
Private credits to Korea								
Banks	1.8	0.7	7.4	11.4	10.0	-9.8	-6.2	1.4
Other	3.8	-0.3	6.6	10.7	15.1	-3.1	-12.3	-3.4
Private credits from Korea								
Banks	-3.2	-4.0	-5.1	-9.2	-8.2	-8.3	7.0	-0.2
Other	0.2	0.1	-1.9	-4.6	-4.7	-5.0	-0.2	-2.1
Net public transactions	-0.9	-2.6	-5.6	-1.0	-1.0	4.5	4.6	3.1
Total[a]	7.0	3.2	10.7	17.3	23.9	-9.2	-8.4	12.7

Source: International Monetary Fund (IMF), *International Financial Statistics*, Washington, November 2000.
a. Excludes capital transfers.
b. Provisional figures.

who dumped Korean stock even when doing so meant taking a big hit. As the stock market fell, so did the international value of the won. The exchange rate depreciation, in turn, caused many banks and firms to become technically bankrupt, since their assets were insufficient to cover their liabilities.

The case of Taiwan is quite different. Taiwan did not experience large capital inflows, not because foreign investors and lenders were not interested in Taiwan, but because the authorities did not allow it to happen. Although Taiwan underwent a process of domestic financial liberalization and limited opening of the capital account in the 1990s, that process was extremely cautious. Capital inflows are still strictly regulated. Given Taiwan's long-standing current account surplus, the authorities gave priority to liberalizing capital outflow.

Taiwan limits the value of shares that can be held by foreigners: any single foreigner may hold up to 15 percent of a listed company's equity, and all foreigners together may hold up to 30 percent. Acquisitions of Taiwanese companies by foreigners are forbidden.[35] On the other hand, there are no restrictions on greenfield FDI investments, profit remittances, or the repatriation of capital. Foreign institutional investors have a ceiling of U.S.$600 million on the investments they can make in Taiwan. Natural foreign persons can purchase up to U.S.$5 million in Taiwanese assets, and firms that are not listed institutional investors face a ceiling of U.S.$50 million. As already noted, Taiwanese banks are under the strict guidance and supervision of the Central Bank as regards their taking on foreign liabilities for conversion into N.T. dollar–denominated assets. The use of N.T. dollar derivatives is authorized by the Central Bank only for genuine hedging purposes. For example, cross-currency swaps between the N.T. dollar and the U.S. dollar may be used to cover bank loan obligations or interest payments from one currency to another in order to hedge currency and interest rate risks.

With regard to capital outflows, the use of foreign exchange for overseas investment is allowed, but such investments must be approved by the Ministry of Economic Affairs and the Central Bank. Natural persons may invest up to U.S.$5 million abroad without permission. The limit for a domestic firm is U.S.$50 million.

It might be objected that the current account surplus is evidence that greater capital account liberalization would not have led to stronger capi-

---

35. Judging from press reports, this norm appears to have been liberalized in 1999.

tal inflows. Stronger capital inflows are certainly compatible with a surplus on current account. Had they taken place, foreign investments in the Taiwanese economy would have been even greater and the outflows of capital from Taiwan even larger. Larger capital inflows, however, would have made Taiwan more vulnerable to the type of events that took place in Korea. Had Taiwan been more open to capital inflows, the effects of the crisis undoubtedly would have been far worse. Taiwan is one of the most successful economies in the world. It has strong companies that might be of interest to many transnational corporations. Its stock market is undoubtedly attractive for institutional investors and individuals looking for plays in emerging markets. Many Taiwanese banks might have borrowed more had the monetary authorities allowed them to do so.[36] They might have used the good credit rating of Taiwan to borrow and lend in other countries, much as the Korean banks did.

The fact is that none of the damaging sequence of events that took place in Korea happened in Taiwan. The main cause for Taiwan's relative success is clearly its much more cautious policy on the kinds of capital inflow that are likely to lead to those situations. At the time of the crisis, Taiwan's external debt was notably low at about U.S.$25 billion, a figure that is insignificant in comparison to its international reserves (see table 2-5). Most of its debt was in the form of trade credit. In other words, Taiwan had low levels of external indebtedness because it was cautious about borrowing excessively. Equity markets had little foreign investment, so portfolio outflows were commensurately moderate after the crisis struck.

Korea, on the other hand, found itself in a situation of extreme financial fragility shortly after liberalizing short-term capital inflows. By 1996, just three years after the implementation of the most ambitious measures, the ratio of short-term debt to reserves had reached a level that was not macroeconomically sustainable, which should have alerted the authorities. The increase in the ratio was not the result of a fall in reserves, which had in fact risen; it was due entirely to a very rapid accumulation of short-term debt. Large inflows of portfolio capital also meant that the country had made itself very vulnerable to a change in sentiment. And that is what happened: before the crisis became full-blown, most of the foreign investors in Korean stock had already exited.

---

36. Taiwanese interest rates are lower than those in Korea, however, so the possibilities for arbitrage are more limited.

The Role of Contagion

Contagion clearly had a leading role in the Korean debacle. Would the crisis have occurred in the absence of contagion? Probably not. If measured on the basis of pre-crisis levels for the exchange rate and interest rates, major Korean firms and banks were not insolvent. Banks were certainly vulnerable to a liquidity squeeze, and the *chaebol* were vulnerable to a slowdown in world demand for their products, but both banks and firms would have been able to resolve their problems if foreign investors had been willing to keep their money in Korea and creditors had rolled over expiring loans, even at higher interest rates. The proper role of the IMF should have been to coordinate expectations around the fact that Korean institutions were solvent. By insisting that major structural changes were required, it reinforced the view of market participants that something was fundamentally wrong with the economy, its firms, and its banks.

Korea clearly had better fundamentals than, say, Thailand or Malaysia. As noted, Korea's current account deficit was significant only in 1996 (4.4 percent of GDP). For the period 1992–96, the average Korean deficit was a mere 1.6 percent. And even in 1996, Korea's deficit was well below Thailand's (7.9 percent of GDP). Thailand ran an average current account deficit of 6.5 percent of GDP for the period 1992–96. The average deficit for Malaysia in the same period was 5.8 percent of GDP, with a peak of 9.7 percent in 1995.[37]

International financial markets worried about Korea only after the onset of the financial crisis elsewhere. Before the crisis struck other East Asian countries, international portfolio investors and international banks were pouring finance into the Korean economy. After the Thai, Malaysian, and Indonesian crises, they reassessed their commitments to Korea and pulled out en masse, with all the adverse consequences described above. The almost unrestricted opening of the capital account (following over three decades of universally acclaimed economic success) made the country highly vulnerable to just such a sequence of events.

Korea experienced several forms of contagion, starting with the effect on trade. Generally speaking, when a crisis affects real economies, other countries experience a drop in export volumes or export prices or both. In the Korean case, export prices had worsened before the onset of the crisis

37. Data drawn from International Monetary Fund, *International Financial Statistics*, various issues.

as a consequence of the insufficient demand vis-à-vis a huge increase in supply, partly because the *chaebols* insisted on going ahead with their investment plans regardless of world market conditions.

The second important form of contagion was financial contagion. A financial crisis in one country can spread to other economies if the ensuing panic causes investors to flee and creditors to refuse to roll over credit. This was the major form of contagion in the Korean case, and the one that produced the most damage to the domestic economy.

The third common manifestation of contagion is in the exchange rate, which occurs when foreign and domestic agents dump the domestic currency and purchase foreign exchange in response to a financial crisis elsewhere. Korea experienced this type of contagion, but it was relatively short-lived. The foreign exchange market witnessed enormous overshooting. The permanent effect was a depreciation of the won from about W 888 to the U.S. dollar before the crisis (at the end of the second quarter of 1997) to about W 1,100 in October 2000. This represents a permanent nominal depreciation of about 25 percent. In real terms, the depreciation was less than 20 percent. This, of course, reflects the inefficiency of financial markets. The Korean won was overvalued in mid-1997, but it did not need to go through the wild gyrations that it experienced between the fourth quarter of 1997 and the end of 1998.

Taiwan similarly experienced strong trade contagion, which was expressed in a sharp fall in the growth rate of export volumes. Some degree of exchange rate contagion was also felt, but it was much milder than in Korea. As already noted, most of the nominal exchange rate depreciation that occurred in Taiwan in late 1997 was quickly corrected. Where Taiwan really differs from Korea is in the area of financial contagion: Taiwan experienced no such phenomenon. The country had little volatile foreign capital within its borders, so little fled. If Taiwanese individuals and companies wished to leave, their ability to do so was limited by financial regulations.

Concluding Remarks

The main lesson to be drawn from the differing experiences of Korea and Taiwan is that liberalization of the capital account of the balance of payments needs to be very cautious, particularly when it comes to short-term flows and portfolio capital. Countries that choose to liberalize must, at the very least, ensure that banking supervision and regulation are adequate. Since domestic interest rates in emerging economies are bound to be higher than international rates, domestic banks operating in economies with a high degree of integration into international financial markets are under constant temptation to borrow abroad. Preventing major mismatches requires strong, well-trained supervisory authorities. This is easier said than done. Good banking regulation and supervision develop gradually and are highly correlated with the level of development. Their evolution is often speeded, however, as a consequence of a financial crisis. Korea is likely to come out of the crisis with a much improved domestic financial system, much as Chile did after its 1982 banking crisis.

But better banking supervision is not a panacea. In financially open economies where banks are not allowed to borrow freely, domestic firms that can borrow directly from international markets may take on excessive international debt.[38] When times are good and the real exchange rate is appreciating, even rational firms may simply ignore the possibility of a damaging exchange rate depreciation. Unhedged borrowing by firms was a component in the Korean and other financial crises of the late 1990s. Since the borrowing by each firm inflicts an adverse externality on the economy as a whole (by exposing it to the risk that changes in creditor and investor sentiment will force many firms into bankruptcy), there is a good argument for monitoring such borrowings and limiting it when necessary.[39]

Large capital inflows may have other adverse effects on the economy, as well. Large inflows unleash asset price bubbles that could attract even more foreign capital, which is extremely volatile and can thus cause excessive fluctuations in the real exchange rate. Such fluctuations are highly damaging in countries that are attempting to integrate into international markets through trade. A good part of these flows is temporary, but they can have permanent effects on recipient economies. It may therefore be advisable for the authorities to limit them. This is precisely what Taiwan has done—and what Korea used to do before 1992. Korea has now dismantled most of its controls on capital inflows, however. Much of this process was carried out

38. This point is made forcefully by Furman and Stiglitz (1998).

39. Fischer (1998), a fervent advocate of capital account liberalization, suggests that prudential controls ought to include matching requirements on nonbank firms' assets and liabilities in foreign exchange.

before the crisis struck, and the authorities have essentially completed that task as a result of the crisis, partly under pressure from the IMF. The policy apparatus that allowed the country to change its economic structure dramatically and to build strong, internationally competitive firms is now gone.

The firms are still there, however, and the Korean economy is recovering from the crisis much faster than anyone expected. The growth of the Korean economy was very strong in 1999 (almost 11 percent), and despite a slowdown in the fourth quarter, it appears to have exceeded 8 percent in 2000. Much of the growth in 1999 and 2000 represents a recovery of consumption and equipment investment. The Central Bank was able to reduce interest rates as international reserves recovered and capital began to flow back in, which was very beneficial to the highly-leveraged Korean corporate sector. Strong export growth has also assisted the recovery.

Nonetheless, the crisis is forcing major changes on the Korean economy. The banking sector is undergoing a profound transformation, and it is to be hoped that banking regulation and supervision will advance significantly. On the other hand, the Korean authorities have been forced to open the economy to the purchase of domestic firms by foreign interests. There are reports of large inflows of FDI, mainly in the form of M&A. Many financial and nonfinancial firms are being bought up at bargain-basement prices by investment funds—and often not by transnational corporations in the same field as the acquired companies, which could be expected to contribute new management or technology. The purchasers are portfolio investors rather than long-term direct investors, and they are likely to hold on to their Korean assets only until their prices rise with the consolidation of economic recovery.

Recovery has thus stimulated renewed capital inflows. Korean firms are already regaining their access to international financial markets. Foreign funds are returning to the stock market. Korean banks will take longer to regain international creditworthiness, since the bank restructuring process is far from complete.[40] It is to be hoped that the Korean authorities will soon have in place the banking regulation and supervision that can control unnecessary and potentially damaging capital inflow. It is also to be hoped that they will find substitutes for the now discarded capital account controls of the past.

40. Park (1999).

References

Amsden, A. H. 1989. *Asia's Next Giant: South Korea and Late Industrialization.* Oxford University Press.

APEC (Asia-Pacific Economic Cooperation). 1998. *The Impact of Investment Liberalization in APEC: Policy Reviews and Case Studies.* Report by the Economic Committee. Sydney.

Chang, H.-J. 1998. "South Korea: The Misunderstood Crisis." In *Tigers in Trouble: Financial Governance, Liberalisation and Crises in East Asia,* edited by K. S. Jomo. London: Zed Books.

Dean, J. 1998. "Why Left-Wing Moralists and Right-Wing Academics Are Wrong about Asia." *Challenge* (March-April): 44–60.

Eatwell, J. 1997. "International Financial Liberalization: The Impact on World Development." ODS Discussion Paper D-12. New York: United Nations Development Program (UNDP), Office of Development Studies.

Feldstein, M. 1998. "Refocusing the IMF." *Foreign Affairs* (March-April).

Fischer, S. 1998. "Capital Account Liberalization and the Role of the IMF." In *Should the IMF Pursue Capital-Account Convertibility?,* edited by S. Fischer and others. *Essays in International Finance* 207. Princeton University, International Economics Section.

Furman, J., and J. E. Stiglitz. 1998. "Economic Crises: Evidence and Insights from East Asia." *BPEA 2:1998.*

Huang. Y. 1998. "Reflections on Taiwan's Economic Investment Policy Following the Asian Currency Crisis." In *The Asian Currency Crisis: The Taiwan Experience,* edited by C. Mai. Taipei: Chung-Hua Institution for Economic Research.

Kregel, J. 1998a. "Derivatives and Global Capital Flows: Applications to Asia." *Integración y Desarrollo* (February-March): 26–30. Lima.

———. 1998b. "East Asia Is Not Mexico: The Difference between Balance of Payments Crises and Debt Deflation." In *Tigers in Trouble: Financial Governance, Liberalisation and Crises in East Asia,* edited by K. S. Jomo. London: Zed Books.

Noland, M. 1996. "Restructuring Korea's Financial Sector for Greater Competitiveness." APEC Working Paper 96-14. Washington: Institute for International Economics (IIE).

Park, J.-J. 1998. "Financial Crisis in Korea: Why It Happened and How It Can Be Overcome." Seoul: Bank of Korea. Mimeographed.

Park, Y. C. 1996. "The Republic of Korea's Experience with Managing Foreign Capital Flows." In *The Tobin Tax: Coping with Financial Volatility,* edited by M. ul Haq, I. Kaul, and I. Grunberg. Oxford University Press.

———. 1998. "The Financial Crisis in Korea and Its Lessons for Reform of the International Financial System." In *Regulatory and Supervisory Challenges in a New Era of Global Finance,* edited by J. J. Teunissen. The Hague: Forum on Debt and Development (FONDAD).

———. 1999. "The Banking Reform in Korea: Issues and Challenges." Korea University at Seoul. Mimeographed.

PECC (Pacific Economic Cooperation Council). 2000. *Pacific Economic Outlook, 2000–01.* Canberra: Asia Pacific Press at Australian National University.

Radelet, S., and J. Sachs. 1998. "The East Asian Financial Crisis: Diagnosis, Remedies, Prospects." *BPEA 1:1998,* 1–90.

Shim, S. 1998. "Recent Trends and Macroeconomic Forecast for 1998/99." Seoul: Korea Development Institute. Mimeographed.

Taylor, L. 1999. "Lax Public Sector, Destabilizing Private Sector: Origins of Capital Market Crises." In *International Monetary and Financial Issues for the 1990s*, vol. 10, edited by the United Nations Conference on Trade and Development (UNCTAD), 131–55. New York.

Wade, R. 1990. *Governing the Market: Economic Theory and the Role of Government in East Asian Industrialization*. Princeton University Press.

Wang, Y., and H. Zang. 1999. *Adjustment Reforms in Korea Since the Financial Crisis*. Seoul: Korea Institute for International Economic Policy.

World Bank. 1993. *The Asian Miracle: Economic Growth and Public Policy*. Oxford University Press.

Yanagihara, T. 1999. "Regional Policy Coordination in Asia." Paper prepared for the workshop, *Entering the 21st Century: The Changing Development Landscape*, Tokyo. World Bank and Foundation for Advanced Studies in Development (FASID) (26–27 May).

Yang, Y. 1998. "Reflections on the ROC's Financial Policies in Response to the Asian Currency Crisis." In *The Asian Currency Crisis: The Taiwan Experience*, edited by C. Mai. Taipei: Chung-Hua Institution for Economic Research.

RICARDO FFRENCH-DAVIS
HERIBERTO TAPIA*

3

Three Varieties of Capital Surge Management in Chile

Chile's recent history includes three interesting epi-sodes that shed light on the policies designed to confront surges of capital inflows and their effect on the national econ-omy. The first episode began in the mid-1970s and ended with the 1982 debt crisis; the second began in the early 1990s and continued through the so-called Mexican tequila crisis; and the third consisted of the two years preceding the Asian crisis. The three have features in common: they all originated in an overabundance of foreign funds; the capital flew into the private sector; in all cases Chile exhibited some strong fundamentals, such as a fiscal surplus, and held an outstanding image as a successful country; and each financial boom was followed by an international financial crisis. Notable differences, however, are found in both the policy approach used to face the capital flood in the three cases and the results obtained. The three cases thus offer a valuable opportunity to study the relation between the economic policies in question and their consequences.[1]

This paper focuses on the characteristics of the three booms and their impact on the sustainability of macroeconomic balances. It is during this

*We are grateful to Guillermo Le Fort, Manuel Marfán, Carlos Massad, Jaime Ros, Gonzalo San-hueza, John Williamson, Felipe Jiménez, Daniel Titelman, María Ángela Parra, and Andras Uthoff for substantive comments and criticisms.
1. See Ffrench-Davis (2001, chaps. 5, 6, and 10).

stage of the cycle that future crises are seeded or avoided. We only marginally consider the post-boom period, when additional shocks (such as on the terms of trade) may affect the adjustment path of the economy.

The impact of capital flows on emerging economies can be analyzed in two dimensions. The first refers to the capacity for domestic absorption, which largely determines how flows affect fundamentals in the host country. If absorption is efficient, capital inflows will contribute to a sustainable growth process. If, on the contrary, the new funds distort key macroeconomic prices, then wrong resource allocation results, and external saving will crowd out national saving. The central issue here is how to extract the benefits from a higher availability of capital. The second dimension has to do with external vulnerability. It involves examining the economy's exposure as it encounters volatile financial markets in order to determine the cost of instability. Both dimensions are crucial for assessing the management of capital flows. Dealing with the first is a necessary—but not sufficient—condition for sound financial integration, while neglecting the second may generate considerable short-term benefits at the cost of medium-term risks stemming from higher foreign debt and exchange rate and current account imbalances. These factors send the wrong signals to the productive sector and ultimately make the economy the victim of its own success.

Chile was the recipient of huge capital flows in each of the three periods under consideration. Private sector capital predominated in all three cases, and it was directed to Chile's private sector. However, indicators of vulnerability, such as the current account deficit and an appreciated exchange rate, and indicators of sound domestic absorption, such as national saving and investment rates and the growth rate of potential gross domestic product (GDP), behaved differently in each case. The first case in the 1970s coincided with low domestic investment and saving. Foreign saving sharply crowded out national saving, and the macroeconomic environment —with an appreciated exchange rate and extremely high interest rates— discouraged the channeling of resources to productive investment. GDP growth was high for several years, however, because the large underutilized capacity resulting from the heavy 1975 recession (when GDP fell 13 percent) left an important margin for easy economic recovery. In other words, GDP was able to grow without requiring new capital formation. Rapid expansion of aggregate demand, stimulated by financial capital inflows, thus moved the economy toward its productive frontier, closing the gap by

1980–81.[2] The large indebtedness made the economy highly vulnerable to external shifts, but it was also in itself unsustainable, given a current account deficit of 14.5 percent of GDP in 1981 (at current prices; the figure is 21 percent with a normalized dollar) and growing amounts coming due. Pronounced inefficiencies thus characterized both the absorption of flows (which was mainly limited to contributing to the recovery of economic activity) and management of the external vulnerability. The result was that in 1982 Chile suffered the deepest debt crisis of all Latin American countries.

The situation was entirely different in the first half of the 1990s, reflecting the lessons learned. GDP grew strongly and was accompanied by high investment and saving. The pre-tequila phase in Chile, unlike the period preceding the debt crisis, began with high utilization of productive capacity. Policy designed to maintain the stability of macroeconomic prices allowed aggregate demand to increase along with saving and investment. The high growth rates were therefore sustainable over time. In other words, capital inflows were absorbed efficiently. In the external sector, the current account deficit was carefully controlled, and the Central Bank pursued an active policy of preventing excessive exchange rate appreciation. With the Mexican crisis of 1994–95, the Chilean economy showed that its domestic achievements were accompanied by great strengths on the external front. A positive trade shock reinforced this solid position.

Chile was highly regarded in the international community at the start of the third episode. The economy had been almost immune to contagion from the tequila effect, and it enjoyed full utilization of capacity and solid domestic fundamentals. In 1996–97 Chile recorded vigorous growth that could be judged sustainable thanks to high domestic investment rates, but the economy was becoming vulnerable to changes in the international environment. When such changes occurred in 1998, driven by the large trade and financial shocks brought on by the Asian crisis, Chile had a high external deficit and an appreciated exchange rate. The country was forced to undergo an intense process of macroeconomic adjustment, which led to a recession (though with a moderate drop in GDP of 1 percent in 1999).

The specific policies and approaches used in each of the three episodes varied, evolving from the extreme naiveté of the 1970s into the more pragmatic approach of the early 1990s. The end of the century saw a turning away from macroeconomic sustainability as authorities gave in to the temp-

2. Ffrench-Davis (2001, chap. 1).

tation to move toward financial globalization without properly respecting underlying risks.

Liberalization of the Capital Account: 1975–82

Shortly after the military coup of 1973, Chile began its transition to a free-market economy with a series of institutional reforms of great depth and breadth. The implementation of the neoliberal model meant substantial changes in the public sector's role in the national economy. An intense program of import liberalization was initiated in 1973, and the financial system was radically reformed in 1975. Almost all the banks that had been nationalized by the previous government were privatized. Interest rates were abruptly deregulated in April 1975, and the rules governing lending (which encouraged its channeling to production rather than consumption) were eliminated. Authorities underrated prudential supervision, believing that the market would do the job.[3]

Volume, Source, and Use of Flows

Capital flows into Chile rose fast starting in 1977 as a result of the boom in lending to developing countries by international banks, which was triggered by the capital surplus of oil-producing countries and was further stimulated by domestic financial reforms. Chile exhibited a significant accumulation of international reserves up to 1981, although shortly thereafter the external sector showed a high and rising current account deficit. The capital flow was overwhelmingly concentrated in the private sector without guarantees by the State, with less than one-fifth of inflows taking the form of foreign direct investment (FDI) and loans to the public sector.

Flows were sizeable in the second half of the 1970s, as shown in table 3-1. Foreign saving (the current account deficit) and debt service also grew as a share of exports, despite very strong export activity in the initial years of the neoliberal experiment. Foreign debt service in 1982 equaled 88 percent of goods and services exports, that is, three times the debt-service coefficient for 1970–74. The magnitude of capital movements is reflected in the fact that for 1980–81, gross loans received climbed to 24 percent of

---

3. See Ffrench-Davis and Arellano (1981); Díaz-Alejandro (1985); Edwards and Cox Edwards (1987); Ffrench-Davis (2001, chap. 5); Harberger (1985); Morandé and Schmidt-Hebbel (1988); Reinstein and Rosende (2000); Tapia (1979); Valdés-Prieto (1992).

Table 3-1. *Chile, Net Capital Inflows, and GDP Growth, 1977–2000*
Percent of GDP

Period	Net capital inflows		Savings (current prices)		Fixed investment (1986 prices)	Actual GDP growth (1986 prices)	Potential GDP growth[b]
	Current prices	1986 prices[a]	National	External			
1977–81	10.8	17.2	11.6	7.2	18.7	7.5	3.0
1982–89	5.5	6.4	11.5	6.2	18.2	2.6	3.0
1990–95	6.9	6.9	22.1	2.5	26.1	7.8	7.0
1996–97	8.0	9.2	21.2	5.7	31.6	7.4	7.1
1998–2000	1.2	1.3	21.6	2.7	28.6	2.7	4.8

Source: Central Bank of Chile. Potential GDP based on R. Ffrench-Davis, *Economic Reforms in Chile: From Dictatorship to Democracy*, chap. 1, University of Michigan Press, 2001.

a. The constant price series was derived by deflating the dollar series using an index of foreign prices faced by the Chilean economy. For the denominator, GDP at constant prices was converted into 1986 dollars using the 1986 peso-dollar exchange rate.

b. Productive capacity created in every period.

GDP. All of these indicators were substantially greater than the Latin American averages for the 1970s.[4]

The composition of agents participating in capital flows changed significantly in this period. On the lending side, 84 percent of the foreign debt in 1981 was to banks, compared to only 19 percent at the end of 1974. Chile's bank debt grew 57 percent a year between 1977 and 1981, while the average for developing countries was 28 percent. On the borrowing side, the growing net inflows were directed primarily at the private sector from 1975 on, while the State moved toward a budget surplus. A deliberate policy of reducing the role of the State was facilitated by changes in international markets, where official institutions lending to governments lost relevance while private capital markets emerged strongly as a source of access for both public and private borrowers.

The great majority of private debt was contracted with no explicit guarantee by the State. Fully two-thirds of Chile's total debt lacked such guarantee in 1981. Through 1977, the private sector obtained a significant part of its loans directly, as a result of quantitative restrictions then applying to local banks with respect to foreign financial credits.[5] From 1978 on, domestic banks were allowed gradually greater importance in the direct intermediation of foreign financing. It was only in April 1980, however, that domestic banks were allowed access to foreign credit on the same conditions as the nonbanking sector. Lending through the banking sector grew dramatically from then on, yet flows to the nonfinancial sector continued to grow at a significant rate as well. The private sector received 94 percent of the gross flow in 1976–81.[6]

Debt and Macroeconomic Adjustment

Chile took on massive quantities of debt between 1977 and 1981, which had significant effects on aggregate demand and its composition. It also contributed to both economic recovery and the concentration of wealth, crowded out domestic savings, and had a decisive effect on monetary and exchange rate policies. Generally speaking, the initial impact of foreign borrowing is an increase in the supply of foreign currency, which can lead to two outlets: an increase in reserves or exchange rate appreciation and a growing current account deficit. Chile experienced both effects

---

4. Ffrench-Davis (1984).

5. A large share of these loans was backed by bank guarantees at the beginning of the borrowing boom. See Ffrench-Davis (2001, table 5.4).

6. See Ffrench-Davis (2001, chap. 5).

up to 1981. Net capital inflows were greater than the capacity of the domestic economy to absorb foreign funding, despite the growing expansion of that capacity as a result of economic recovery, import liberalization, and exchange rate revaluations driven by inflows.

The rapid accumulation of reserves, in turn, had substantial effects on the money supply. The large capital flows—both those used to finance increased imports and those that went to expanding international reserves—led to a high proportion of the economy's domestic credit being based on foreign funding. Despite this volume, substantial differences between domestic and external interest rates persisted.

MONETARY POLICY AND CAPITAL CONTROLS   Starting in 1975, net purchases of foreign currency by the Central Bank were the main source of money supply expansion.[7] They represented over 100 percent of money supply changes in the three-year period 1978–80. As already mentioned, the overwhelming share corresponded to private borrowing; operations with the public sector actually had a contractive effect in some years. The severe macroeconomic disequilibria that had been accumulating finally emerged in 1981, when international reserves began to fall. The monetary effect of foreign exchange operations correspondingly became strongly contractive.

Some direct restrictions were applied to capital inflows as a part of the monetary program. One such restriction was designed specifically to moderate the monetary effects of flows by limiting the amount that banks could exchange each month at the Central Bank. This measure was in effect from 1977 to 1979, with a series of modifications in the maximum amount allowed.[8] The restrictions were not sufficient, however, to hold foreign loans to the private sector at a volume consistent with the rate of monetary expansion considered desirable by economic authorities. Domestic credit by the Central Bank (rediscounts or loans to the banking sector) was therefore tightened in the face of increased money supply stemming from foreign exchange dealings. Nevertheless, the increase in aggregate demand was much more rapid than GDP growth. A strong real exchange rate revaluation took place despite the accumulation of reserves, which had the effect of crowding out domestic producers of tradables.

Targets for expanding liquidity were in effect while a closed-economy approach predominated in policymaking. In 1979, authorities adopted an

7. Ffrench-Davis and Arellano (1981, table 13).
8. Ffrench-Davis and Arellano (1981).

open-economy monetary approach to the balance of payments. The nominal exchange rate was frozen in June, and a supposedly neutral monetary policy was established. Variations in the level of international reserves were to automatically determine the economy's level of liquidity, within the context of a fiscal budget in surplus and low reserve ratios in the banking sector.

In April 1979, an unremunerated reserve requirement was established for foreign loans (under Article 14), with percentages varying according to the term of the loan. The prohibition on loans with an average maturity of less than twenty-four months was maintained (with a 100 percent reserve requirement), and reserve requirements were based on a structure of decreasing rates according to the loan term. Loans over sixty-six months were exempt. In August 1979 and July 1980, rates were lowered for loans with a maturity of over twenty-four months. The modifications were not significant for two reasons, however. First, no loan of less than two years could be contracted throughout this period, except for trade credits governed by limits that had survived the deregulation of April 1980. Second, the strong segment of the international market at the time was syndicated loans, whose average term varied from six to ten years in 1976–80.[9]

The monetary approach to the balance of payments prevailed from mid-1979 to mid-1982, with a neutral monetary policy based on the dollar standard. At the end of these three years, a contractionary automatic adjustment was in effect, with disastrous results on employment and output.[10]

EXCHANGE RATE POLICY   Exchange rate policy evolved significantly in the 1974–82 period.[11] Up to June 1976, there was a crawling-peg regime, with adjustments made one to four times a month. The subsequent regime combined daily devaluations determined each month in advance with four abrupt changes in the value of foreign currency (two devaluations and two revaluations). In early 1978 and 1979, a table of daily adjustments was established for the remainder of each year. In June 1979, this system was interrupted with a devaluation that brought the price of the dollar to the level scheduled for the end of the year (39 pesos). This rate was maintained until June 1982, when there was an 18 percent devaluation and an announcement of a table of smaller devaluations. This was soon replaced, however, by a short-lived freely floating exchange rate, which was followed by a return to a crawling-peg regime. The evolution of the real exchange rate is shown in figure 3-1.

9. Ffrench-Davis (1984, table 11).
10. See Arellano and Cortázar (1982); Ffrench-Davis (2001, chaps. 1 and 4).
11. See Ffrench-Davis (2001, chap. 4).

Figure 3-1. *Real Exchange Rate, 1974–2000* [a]

Index, 1974 = 100

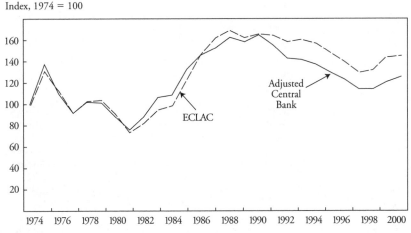

Source: United Nations Economic Commission for Latin America and the Caribbean (ECLAC); Central Bank of Chile; Ffrench-Davis (2001).

Net inflows were a crucial factor in making it possible for the authorities to manage the exchange rate with goals other than efficient resource allocation until 1981. The use of the exchange rate to shape expectations (in 1976–79) or to anchor domestic prices to external prices (1979–82) resulted in lower inflation, but it also produced significant real exchange rate appreciation (45 percent between 1975 and 1981). When combined with import liberalization (the average tariff was reduced from 94 percent to 10 percent) and the economic recovery of 1977–81, this caused the notable current account deficit mentioned above.[12] Furthermore, the gradual appreciation brought the observed real cost of foreign borrowing down to negative levels in 1979 and 1980, which encouraged inflows.

INTEREST RATE DIFFERENTIALS　The government expected liberalization to cause a strong trend toward the reduction of spreads, with an equalizing of domestic and foreign interest rates. Large differentials between lending

12. The increase in the deficit was also associated with high interest payments and falling copper prices. The loss in government revenue in 1981—compared to the 1965–70 average—represented 1.6 percent of GDP. The sharp fall in copper prices was partially offset by the government's capturing the economic rent following the nationalization of copper mining in successive stages in 1966, 1969, and 1971.

Table 3-2. *Chile: Domestic and External Real Interest Rates, 1975–82*[a]
Annual percent in pesos

Year	Domestic	External	Differential
1975[b]	121.0	. . .	. . .
1976	51.2	−21.1	72.3
1977	39.4	0.2	39.2
1978	35.1	3.8	31.3
1979	16.9	−0.9	17.8
1980	12.2	−8.0	20.2
1981	38.8	12.4	26.4
1982	35.2	45.0	−9.8

Sources: Author's calculations, based on data from the Central Bank of Chile; Instituto Nacional de Estadísticas (INE); R. Cortázar and J. Marshall, "Indice de precios al consumidor en Chile: 1970–78," *Colección Estudios CIEPLAN* 4 (November), 1980; R. Ffrench-Davis and J. P. Arellano, "Apertura financiera externa: la experiencia chilena en 1973–80," *Colección Estudios CIEPLAN* 5 (July), 1981.

a. The domestic rate refers to the predominant segment of the market, covering transactions for terms of thirty to ninety-one days. The external interest rate is that paid for bank credits obtained under Article 14, plus the cost in respect of compulsory deposits and the financial spread, all converted into their peso equivalents. In 1982 the preferential exchange rate was used to calculate the external interest rate.

b. Second semester, after interest rate liberalization.

and borrowing rates in the domestic financial market persisted throughout the period, however, and both rates were quite high. In addition, domestic rates continued to exceed international rates by a wide margin despite the large capital inflows, especially from 1979 on (see table 3-2).[13]

The distributive impact of interest rate differentials is illustrated by the fact that between 1976 and 1982 the average domestic borrower paid interest exceeding a "normal" annual real rate of 8 percent, equivalent to 300 percent of the principal borrowed. In other words, a borrower who paid the lender 8 percent, renewed principal, and capitalized interest over 8 percent would, by the end of 1982, have had a debt four times the initial one, in currency of constant purchasing power. By contrast, the debtor borrowing abroad on the same terms would have owed 44 percent less be-

13. One recurring explanation is that the rate differentials derived from expectations of devaluation. In 1981, however, many local borrowers still moved from peso-denominated to foreign-denominated debt. Ffrench-Davis (2001, chap. 5), and Harberger (1985) examine the causes of the real interest rate differentials in pesos. These causes were reinforced by the rediscount constraints imposed by the Central Bank.

fore the 1982 devaluation than the original debt contracted in 1976. The massive real devaluation of 80 percent then raised this borrower's debt to its original level (equivalent to only one-fourth of the first borrower's peso-denominated debt). The figures vary, obviously, according to the date of borrowing. For example, late borrowers who took loans denominated in foreign currency in 1981 lost dramatically, given the real devaluations that took place in 1982.

These differentials had significant effects, from both the allocative and distributive points of view.[14] Small and medium-size enterprises (SMEs) were largely relegated to the high-interest segment of the market. Firms associated with the management of financial institutions, as well as the larger economic groups, enjoyed expeditious access to foreign credit, whether directly or through the intermediation of Chilean banks. The low rates of saving and investment during this period show that the environment provided more incentives for financial activity and speculation than for productive activities.[15]

DETERIORATED PORTFOLIO QUALITY AND PRUDENTIAL SUPERVISION   Foreign borrowing gave rise to a domestic lending boom. The increase in credit took several forms: direct foreign loans not backed by guarantees, direct foreign loans with guarantees, foreign loans intermediated by local banks, and loans made by these banks in domestic currency on the basis of the liquidity generated by foreign exchange operations. The lending boom took place in an atmosphere of very lax prudential supervision. Related-party lending rose rapidly, often without guarantees or with fictitious guarantees. Regulations were circumvented via cross-lending and loans to paper firms, as well as loans through off-shore institutions. Faced with high interest rates, the banks renewed loans (often on a thirty-day basis) and financed interest payments with new loans. Meanwhile, the stock of loans grew 38 percent a year in real terms between 1976 and 1981. Nonperforming loans appeared low and the banks' profits high. Many loans were backed by stock and real estate, but the prices of such collateral were inflated as a result of the financial boom and the mistaken belief that the Chilean economy would continue to grow at around 8 percent a year.

Required provisions were low. In 1979, general requirements were re-

14. Zahler (1980).
15. See Mizala (1992).

duced from 2 percent of loans to 0.75 percent. Priority was to be given to individual provisions, although this was not implemented. After the explosion of the banking crisis in January 1983, observers realized that 19 percent of loans in late 1982 were with related parties and represented 249 percent of the capital and reserves of private banks. The severe weakness of the financial system, which resulted from typical neoliberal reforms, had enormous fiscal costs in the following years.[16]

It should be emphasized that around 40 percent of external lending to private firms in the domestic market (Article 14) was handled directly, with no intermediary between borrowers and foreign lenders. Consequently, not even the strictest and most effective prudential supervision of the local financial system could have fully prevented the development of macroeconomic imbalances as a result of the boom in foreign funding.[17]

Inefficient Domestic Absorption and External Vulnerability

The world economy and the domestic market underwent a process of increasing indebtedness, which led to a gradual exchange rate appreciation and great vulnerability for Chile's external sector. The belief that the appreciation would prove sustainable made foreign loans more attractive. Stock and real estate prices were rising at a dizzying rate.[18] Such feedback reinforced the cycle, increasing the inflow of capital. This, in turn, increased aggregate demand and supported the persistent exchange rate appreciation and a notable rise in asset prices. The economy became increasingly accommodated to a massive financial inflow, and aggregate demand became highly intensive in importables.[19]

The form that foreign funding took and the incentives provided by the economic model led to a decrease in investment, and, more so, in national savings (see table 3-1 above).[20] Gross fixed capital formation aver-

16. Held and Jiménez (2001); Sanhueza (1999).

17. See Valdés-Prieto (1992) on the weaknesses of prudential supervision on the supply side and the importance of nonbank flows.

18. The General Stock Price Index grew by 1,000 percent between 1976 and 1980. Real estate prices peaked in 1981 at more than 100 percent above their 1976 prices (Morandé, 1992).

19. Ffrench-Davis and De Gregorio (1987).

20. One theoretical interpretation of the crowding out of national savings is that a sharp rise in productivity generated the expectation that GDP capacity would continue to grow by 8 percent a year even given a low investment ratio. Anticipating the consumption of future increased income was therefore seen as an equilibrating intertemporal adjustment. Since the expectation was wrong—capacity was growing very slowly—the adjustment was actually destabilizing (Ffrench-Davis and Reisen, 1998, chap. 1).

aged only 18.7 percent of GDP in 1977–81, significantly under the 21.2 percent average of the 1960s.[21] A growing share of funds was channeled to the consumption of imported goods, crowding out spending on domestic tradables and national savings. This phenomenon intensified in 1981, as the process of recovery came up against the economy's productive capacity. National savings fell to 8 percent of GDP in 1981 and to 2 percent in 1982. Excessively high domestic interest rates, the dismantling of public mechanisms to support productive activities, the drop in public investment, and an abrupt import liberalization with an appreciated and unstable exchange rate all combined to discourage productive investment.

It was obvious that the external deficit could not be sustained for long, even if the international environment were to remain unchanged. Nevertheless, the government argued that the process was in balance because private lenders were financing it and that it would be self-regulating. Demand for imports would soon reach the saturation point, spontaneously checking the rise. A currency crisis could not occur against a background of budget surpluses, international reserves larger than high-powered money, and a supposedly neutral monetary policy. When international financial problems began to emerge in 1981, however, the current account deficit was 14.5 percent.[22] There was a clear and compelling need to reduce the external imbalance and correct the appreciated exchange rate.

Chile's difficulty in obtaining foreign loans in 1982 coincided, then, with a great domestic need for fresh funds to pay growing interest and amortization costs, as well as to cover the trade deficit. The composition of the foreign debt had some strongly negative dynamics. First, given the prevalence of variable international interest rates, net interest payments quadrupled between 1978 and 1982 (reaching 7 percent of GDP), after the contraction of international financial markets. Second, short-term debt grew from what was considered a normal level, associated with a sustainable volume of trade, to double its share, reaching 20 percent of all debt by 1982

21. Figures in 1986 currency. The authorities reiterated that increased productivity made higher investment unnecessary. Our calculations show, however, that of the actual GDP increase of 6.5 percent in the 1976–80 period, only 2 percent a year was due to increased capacity, while the rest reflected exploitation of existing capacity that had been underused since the deep recession of 1975 (Ffrench-Davis, 2001, chap. 1).

22. This figure, in current prices, underestimates the importance of the deficit as a result of the excessive exchange rate appreciation in 1981. The deficit climbs to 21 percent of GDP if measured using the exchange rate of 1976–78. For a discussion of alternative measures of this coefficient, see Ffrench-Davis (2001, chap. 5).

Table 3-3. *Debt Crisis in Chile, 1977–83*

Indicator	1977	1978	1979	1980	1981	1982	1983
GDP[a]	8.3	7.8	7.1	7.7	6.7	−13.4	−3.5
Aggregate expenditure[a]	12.9	9.7	10.4	10.5	12.4	−23.8	−8.6
Fiscal expenditure[a]	8.8	−18.8	−7.4	−3.2	7.6	16.7	−4.0
Exports[a]	12.0	11.8	14.2	14.5	−9.0	4.5	0.1
Imports[a]	32.4	18.1	23.9	20.7	13.3	−34.0	−17.7
Current account deficit[b]	3.7	5.2	5.4	7.1	14.5	9.2	5.4
Real exchage rate[c]	62.8	69.7	69.7	60.9	51.8	60.1	72.1
Terms-of-trade effect[d]	−0.2	−0.9	1.8	−0.6	−2.2	−0.8	1.6

Source: Based on data from the Central Bank of Chile; F. Larraín, "Public Sector Behavior in a Highly Indebted Country: The Contrasting Chilean Experience, 1970–85," in *The Public Sector and the Latin American Crisis*, edited by F. Larraín and M. Selowsky, San Francisco: ICS Press, 1991; Ffrench-Davis (2001).
   a. Official figures at 1986 constant prices, annual growth (percent).
   b. Current prices, percent of GDP.
   c. Index, 1986 = 100.
   d. Current prices, percent of GDP.

(13 percent of GDP). Third, amortization of private medium-term debt grew rapidly.

In brief, the Government was relying on the automatic functioning of the dollar standard, and the productive apparatus was weak and suffering from overindebtedness. The external shocks of the early 1980s thus found the Chilean economy in a very vulnerable position. The effects of the financial and terms-of-trade shocks were multiplied in the domestic market, with a reduction in aggregate spending of 30 percent and a GDP drop of 17 percent in 1982–83 (see table 3-3). In the midst of this general crisis, many observers failed to analyze the specific policies for capital flow management used in this period. The tools were clearly inadequate for counteracting the crisis. This was not so much the fault of the instruments themselves, however, as of the fact that a small economy was confronting an enormous supply of funds and that very high differentials between domestic and foreign interest rates (about 20 to 30 percentage points) made any sort of inflow profitable.

Active Regulation of Capital Inflows: 1990–95

Latin America began to see renewed inflows of private capital in the late 1980s. Chile was one of the first to attract new funds and was among the countries facing the greatest quantity of inflows in relation to the size of its economy. Recipient countries generally experienced macroeconomic problems stemming from the magnitude of the inflows and their composition, which was prone to volatility.[23]

Chilean policy in the first half of the 1990s represented a significant step toward a more pragmatic approach to macroeconomic management. In brief, policymakers responded to the massive availability of foreign capital by attempting to moderate short-term inflows while keeping the door open to long-term flows. Specifically, an unremunerated reserve requirement was established to raise the cost of bringing in short-term capital; this is a market-based instrument that affects relative costs. Authorities also used exchange rate intervention and monetary sterilization to hold down the appreciation of the real exchange rate in the face of those flows that surpassed the reserve barrier and gave way to the monetary effects of foreign operations. These tools were used in support of a development strategy that encouraged export growth and diversification.

The policy was highly successful, in the sense that in 1991–94 the current account deficit was moderate, the currency appreciated less than in most of the region's countries, and the total short-term external debt was held to a fairly low magnitude. When the Mexican exchange rate crisis exploded in late 1994, the Chilean economy proved immune to contagion (see table 3-4). The country had significantly reduced its vulnerability.

Capital Inflows from 1990 to 1995

The return to democracy in 1990 coincided approximately with the beginning of an episode of abundant foreign capital flowing to emerging economies. Effective private inflows to Chile achieved some importance in 1989; after that date, FDI increased steadily and represented a solid majority of capital inflows in the 1990s (see figure 3-2).[24] A set of active macroeconomic policies was adopted to regulate the capital surge. During this period, productive capacity expanded vigorously, and the economy was running close to full capacity. This was a determining factor in creating a virtuous circle of rapid capital formation.[25]

---

23. See, for instance, Calvo, Leiderman, and Reinhart (1993); Ffrench-Davis and Griffith-Jones (1995).

24. Significant movements began in 1986 in relation to a debt conversion program, but this activity involved debt paper instead of cash flows. See Ffrench-Davis (2001, chap. 7).

25. See Agosin (1998); Ffrench-Davis and Reisen (1998).

Table 3-4. *Tequila Crisis in Chile, 1991–95*

Indicator	1991	1992	1993	1994	1995
GDP[a]	8.0	12.3	7.0	5.7	10.6
Aggregate expenditure[a]	6.2	15.0	10.8	5.5	16.2
Fiscal expenditure[a]	10.4	12.3	7.4	5.6	6.2
Exports[a]	12.4	13.9	3.5	11.6	11.0
Imports[a]	7.0	21.8	14.2	10.1	25.0
Current account deficit[b]	0.3	2.3	5.6	3.0	2.0
Real exchage rate[c]	106.4	97.6	96.9	94.3	88.9
Terms-of-trade effect[d]	0.1	−0.3	−1.9	2.8	2.5

Source: Based on data from the Central Bank of Chile; Dirección de Presupuestos del Ministerio de Hacienda (DIPRES), *Estadísticas de las finanzas públicas: 1990–1999*, Santiago, March 2000; Ffrench-Davis (2001).

a. Official figures at 1986 constant prices, annual growth (percent).
b. Current prices, percent of GDP.
c. Index, 1986 = 100.
d. Current prices, percent of GDP.

Private short-term lending also figured prominently in the capital surge into Latin America in the 1990s. For a country to be the target of interest rate arbitrage, domestic interest rates must exceed international rates by a margin that more than offsets the currency's expected depreciation and the country risk. Such conditions obtained in Chile starting in the early 1990s. On the one hand, in 1992 and 1993, international rates on dollar loans were at their lowest level in thirty years, and though they later rose, they continued to be moderate and remained far below their levels in the 1980s. On the other hand, Chile is a capital-scarce country, with a stock consistent with a GDP of only U.S.$5,000 per capita. Because the scarcity entails a higher price, the interest rate in emerging economies tends to be higher than in developed countries.[26] Monetary policy must keep average real interest rates above international rates to ensure sustainable macroeconomic balances.[27]

Other conditions for interest rate arbitrage also proved favorable to inflows. After a cumulative real depreciation of 130 percent in the 1980s,

26. Our policy implications are consistent with the idea that the fastest growing economies have higher interest rates associated with their GDP growth rates.

27. Chilean authorities increased the structural interest rate differential through a macroeconomic adjustment in 1990, based unilaterally on a substantial rise in the interest rate by the Central Bank (see Ffrench-Davis, 2000, chap. 7).

Figure 3-2. *Composition of Capital Flows, 1980–2000*

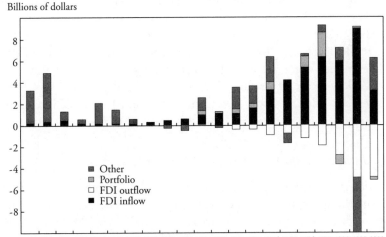

Billions of dollars

Source: Central Bank of Chile.

the exchange rate began to appreciate gradually in the 1990s. As in the case of other countries in the region, Chile's country risk premium fell. An atmosphere of emerging markets mania (à la Kindleberger) on the part of international investors generated a spectacular drop in perceived country risk.[28] Private short-term capital inflows were heavy well into 1992, after which they began to fall as a result of policy measures taken to check them.

Portfolio inflows took two forms: investment through large international mutual funds and the issuing of American depositary receipts (ADRs) by large Chilean firms. Primary issues of ADRs represent an opportunity for a firm to expand its capital at a relatively low cost, since costs in international markets naturally tend to be lower than in the Chilean financial market. Secondary issues of ADRs occur when foreigners purchase securities available on the Chilean stock market and subsequently convert them into ADRs.[29] This operation constitutes a change of ownership from nationals to foreigners, without a direct financial effect on the firm. Chile's relatively developed domestic securities market, together with the growing use of ADRs to reach the U.S. securities market, made Chilean securities

28. For instance, the *Euromoney* index shows an improving country risk from 47.7 in 1990 to 72.9 in 1995.

29. See Ffrench-Davis, Agosin, and Uthoff (1995).

attractive for investors seeking new financial vehicles. These changes of ownership exposed the economy to an additional degree of uncertainty and volatility, since foreign investors can easily withdraw their investments.[30] Such flows clearly played a destabilizing role in the economy. They contributed to the inflationary behavior of the securities market in 1994 and 1997 and depressed the market in 1995 and 1998, operating procyclically.

While private sector flows increased, public debt fell. The Chilean government reduced new credits from international financial institutions and made sizable prepayments, particularly in 1995–96.

The Response of Macroeconomic Policy and Its Effects

Monetary authorities in Chile deployed a wide range of measures to regulate the surge in financial capital in 1990–95. The Central Bank took steps to discourage inflows of short-term, liquid capital by means of the unremunerated reserve requirement. At the same time, it kept the doors open for FDI risk capital. It moderated the impact of those waves of capital by intervening in the foreign exchange market to prevent an overabundance of foreign currency from appreciating the real exchange rate too much and by sterilizing the monetary effects of the rapid accumulation of international reserves.[31]

Three other policies contributed to the success in managing capital inflows. First, fiscal policy was very cautious. Increases in social spending were financed with new taxes. Consequently, Chile had a significant nonfinancial public sector surplus of 1 or 2 percent of GDP. This prudential approach, which included observing the regulations of a stabilization fund for public copper revenues, facilitated the monetary authorities' task of regulating capital inflows, and it contributed to preventing excessive exchange rate appreciation in the first half of the decade. Of course, running a fiscal surplus does not guarantee financial stability. The great 1982 crisis occurred despite Chile's having had several years of budget surpluses. The same thing happened in Mexico with tequila crisis and in Korea with the Asian crisis. In all three cases, the external deficit was led by the private sector.

---

30. Some analysts maintain that foreigners who become pessimistic about a country generally sell their ADRs on the U.S. stock market, and the sale therefore has no impact on domestic stock and foreign exchange markets. This argument disregards the fact that when firms issue ADRs, the prices of securities on the domestic and U.S. markets tend toward equality through arbitrage. In fact, equity price movements of Chilean firms that have issued ADRs on U.S. markets are closely linked with movements on the Santiago exchange.

31. See Ffrench-Davis, Agosin, and Uthoff (1995).

Second, prudential banking regulations had been introduced in response to the banking crisis of 1982–83, and the regulatory system had then been improved over the years. Authorities effectively resisted pressures to weaken supervision when lobbying sectors argued that the system was mature enough to self-regulate; in fact, prudential supervision was strongly intensified. This made it difficult for capital inflows to trigger another credit boom in the commercial banks, which in turn helped keep the current account deficit and exchange rate within sustainable limits until 1995. It is important to note that a significant share of financial flows is not channeled through local banks. This phenomenon became decidedly more pronounced in the 1990s, with the development of portfolio investment funds and derivatives markets. Nevertheless, fiscal responsibility and effective prudential supervision of the financial system are two very important complements in regulating capital flows.

Third, authorities continually monitored aggregate demand and its consistency with productive capacity. Consequently, macroeconomic disequilibria were not allowed to accumulate. Some overheating occurred in 1993, but the authorities conducted a downward adjustment. When the tequila crisis exploded, Chile had a moderate external deficit, large reserves, and space for increasing economic activity. Those conditions would not have been feasible without regulating capital inflows, managing the exchange rate flexibly, and pursuing an active monetary policy.[32]

POLICY FOR MANAGING CAPITAL INFLOWS   Strategic features of the policies used went against the fashion of capital account liberalization. The two main targets of exchange rate and inflows management policies were, first, achieving sustained macroeconomic stability in an economy prone to huge cycles (Chile experienced the sharpest recessions in all Latin America in 1975 and 1982) and, second, supporting the growth model adopted by the authorities, which gave the expansion and diversification of exports a crucial role.

In the face of a plentiful supply of foreign funds, Chilean authorities opted to regulate the foreign currency market in order to prevent large misalignments in the real exchange rate relative to its medium-term trend. The natural short-term horizon of financial markets can lead to exchange rate values that are inconsistent with medium- and long-run trends, which

32. Good luck also played a role, with a sharp improvement in the terms of trade in 1995. Even so, the other factors provided strong macroeconomic insurance.

negatively affects decisions in the productive sector.[33] The authorities sought to preserve the predominance of medium-term fundamentals over short-term factors influencing the exchange rate.

In June 1991, the financial environment featured accelerating growth in available external funds and a high copper price—factors considered to have a significant transitory component. The authorities reacted by establishing an unremunerated reserve requirement of 20 percent on foreign credit (covering the entire spectrum of foreign credit, from that associated with FDI to trade credit). The reserve was to be on deposit at the Central Bank for a minimum of 90 days and a maximum of one year, according to the time frame of the operation. At the same time, a tax on domestic loans of 1.2 percent for operations of up to one year was extended to foreign loans. The reserve requirement, an option of paying its financial cost, and the tax on foreign credits all involved zero marginal cost for the loans outstanding after a one-year term. The first two, however, were heavily onerous for very short-term inflows.

Since capital inflows persisted, the reserve requirement was tightened and extended to almost all international financial transactions. In May 1992 the requirement was raised to 30 percent and was extended to cover time deposits in foreign currency, and in July 1995 it was extended to the purchase of Chilean stocks (secondary ADRs) by foreigners.[34] The term of the deposit was raised to one year, independent of the maturity of the loan. With some lag, authorities took measures to eliminate a loophole that made it possible to circumvent the reserve requirement by means of FDI (since risk capital was exempt). This was accomplished by scrutinizing FDI applications. Permission for FDI exemptions from reserve requirements was denied when it was determined that the inflow was disguised financial capital. In these cases, foreign investors had to register their funds at the Central Bank as financial investments subject to the reserve requirement.

Beginning in 1991, measures were put in place to facilitate capital outflows as a way of lightening pressure on the exchange rate.[35] Specifically, a series of incremental changes allowed Chilean pension funds to invest up

---

33. Ffrench-Davis (2000, chap. 6); Ffrench-Davis and Ocampo (in this volume); Zahler (1998).

34. It is not difficult to impose reserve requirements on foreign portfolio investments. If funds to be invested are deposited in a Chilean bank, they remain subject to the reserve requirement there. For funds not using a Chilean bank as an intermediary, the reserve requirement can be enforced at the time the asset is registered to a party with a foreign address. Registration with the Central Bank is also necessary when converting securities into ADRs.

35. See Ffrench-Davis, Agosin, and Uthoff (1995).

to 6 percent of their total assets abroad as of 1995.[36] Expeditious access to the formal foreign currency market was provided for residents wanting to invest abroad (chapter XII of the exchange regulations), which had the additional benefit of encouraging the development of Chilean firms. This was effective in stimulating considerable flows of FDI, as well as acquisitions by Chilean firms in neighboring countries.[37] Still, the greater profitability of financial assets in Chile compared to financial investments abroad, along with expectations of an appreciating exchange rate, discouraged foreign investments by pension funds and by the mutual funds created at that time.

The immediate effect of deregulating outflows was probably to encourage new inflows thanks to the greater certainty that it gave potential investors coming into Chile. This scenario may actually produce the opposite of the desired effect, because the market takes advantage of the opportunity to move foreign currency abroad when expectations of appreciation are replaced by expectations of depreciation, which is precisely when the economy is most vulnerable and likely to suffer from speculative attack.[38] The progressive deregulation of outflows can thus imply a risk of capital flight not only from the sudden exit of capital that previously came in, but also from domestic funds seeking to speculate against the peso. This procyclical feature makes it particularly dangerous to facilitate outflows by domestic investors, since it weakens the effect of measures such as the reserve requirement on inflows, as was proved in 1998–99.

EXCHANGE RATE POLICY   Exchange rate policy also underwent a substantial shift after the 1982–83 crisis. From 1984 on, authorities used a crawling band, which was widened to ±5 percent in 1989. The official rate was devalued daily, according to an estimate of net inflation. Discrete nominal devaluations were added at various junctures, serving to achieve the notable real depreciation of 130 percent between 1982 and 1988.

Chile was thus coming out of the depths of a debt crisis faced with depreciation. The real exchange rate had reached historic highs, such that there was room for some appreciation. However, the economy was moving from a shortage to a very abundant supply of foreign savings, and authorities wanted to avoid an excessive and overly rapid adjustment in the

---

36. It was argued that this would contribute to diversifying risk and increasing the profitability of the private pension system.

37. Calderón and Griffith-Jones (1995).

38. Williamson (1992); Labán and Larraín (1997).

exchange rate.[39] One particularly problematic aspect of the situation involved foreign expectations: as pessimism turns to optimism, foreign investors tend to rapidly define a new stock of desired investments in the
emerging market; this generates excessive inflows of capital, whose high
levels are naturally transitory, not permanent.

The crawling band was broadened to ±10 percent in January 1992.
This produced a wave of revaluatory expectations fed by capital inflows.
The flows were stimulated by the knowledge that the Central Bank would
not intervene within the set band. For many months, a proposal had cir-
culated at the Central Bank to initiate a dirty or regulated float within the
band. Proponents of such intramarginal intervention argued that given an
increasingly active informal foreign exchange market and a more porous
formal market, the current pure band led to an observed exchange rate
with a tendency toward the extremes of the band (the ceiling in 1989–90,
the floor shortly thereafter). The sudden revaluation of almost 10 percent
in the observed rate between January and February 1992 contributed to
the Bank's initiating the dirty float in March. The observed rate then fluctuated within a range of 1 to 8 points above the floor of the band—in
other words, generally off the bottom of the band and always with active
purchases by the Bank, though also with sales from time to time.

The initial broadening of the band had created expectations that the
Bank had renounced the attempt to avoid revaluatory pressures and sustain the export strategy, instead giving the market—which was dominated
by short-term participants—the job of determining the observed rate
within a very wide range. By establishing the regulated float, the Central
Bank regained a greater role, which allowed it to strengthen the long-term
variables that determine the exchange rate facing producers of exportables
and importables.

In subsequent months, U.S. interest rates continued to fall, putting
pressure on the Central Bank. Nevertheless, the Chilean economy had a
notable boom, with a GDP increase firmly in the double digits. The Bank
therefore wanted to raise rather than lower domestic interest rates to promote macroeconomic balance. To deter arbitrage, it decided to increase the
reserve requirement on capital inflows. The effectiveness of the reserve requirement and its flexible application at that juncture facilitated monetary
policy and avoided accumulation of macroeconomic imbalances.

Finally, in July 1992, the dollar was replaced by a basket of currencies

39. See Zahler (1998).

as the currency standard for the exchange rate. This measure was intended to introduce greater exchange rate uncertainty in short-term dollar-based operations, thereby reducing incentives for interest rate arbitrage, given the daily instability governing the international values of the currencies included (namely, the dollar, the deutsche mark, and the yen). At the same time, replacing the dollar with the basket meant greater stability for average peso values of returns on exports. Unlike financial operations, which are denominated largely in dollars, trade is geographically diversified and thus operates with a more diverse mix of currencies.

The actual market performance strongly indicates that the exchange rate appreciation during this period represented equilibrating movements. This is consistent both with the disappearance of the effects of the 1980s crisis, allowing the elimination of the overdevaluation then required, and with net improvements of productivity for Chilean tradables. A revealed proof is the fact that the current account deficit was very moderate: 2.5 percent GDP in 1990–95.

STRONGER BANKING SUPERVISION The Chilean banking crisis of 1981–86, which followed on the heels of a massive capital surge in the late 1970s, carried a number of valuable lessons that were reflected in Chilean legislation.[40] Some of the elements of prudential supervision adopted include the continuous monitoring of the quality of bank assets; strict limits on banks' lending to related agents; automatic mechanisms to adjust banks' capital when its market value falls beneath thresholds set by regulators; and the authority to freeze bank operations, prevent troubled banks from transferring funds to third parties, and restrict dividend payments by institutions not complying with capital requirements. Chile's financial markets had also become deeper; this allowed the orderly infusion of new funds, as well as their withdrawal, without significantly affecting the quality of bank portfolio.[41]

Despite the quality of prudential supervision, however, macroeconomic imbalances that suddenly lead to massive devaluations and very high interest rates can unexpectedly affect the quality of banks portfolios, as can exploding bubbles in asset markets. Sustainable macroeconomic balances are an essential partner of sustainable prudential supervision.

40. See Díaz-Alejandro (1985); Held and Jiménez (2001); Reinstein and Rosende (2000); Valdés-Prieto (1992).
41. C. Larraín (1995); Aninat and Larraín (1996).

Effectiveness of Policies for Stabilizing Macroeconomic Variables

The Chilean mechanism for prudential macroeconomic regulation attracted considerable international attention, and many studies attempt to measure its effectiveness.[42] Various tests seek to determine how the reserve requirement affects the composition and volume of flows, as well as their impact on the exchange rate, the authorities' ability to make monetary policy, and the aggregate demand. There is ample evidence that Chile's regulations on foreign capital changed the maturity structure of inflows, reducing the short-term component.[43] This evidence points to a very positive feature of the instrument, since the liquidity of foreign liabilities is a major factor in the probability and severity of crises.[44]

Disagreement arises, however, on the effect of the overall volume of flows, since some econometric studies fail to find that these instruments affected the total volume or exchange rates, though they do find an effect on the composition of flows.[45] The implication here is a high substitution between short- and long-term flows. Part of this compensatory phenomenon between flows of different maturities is to be expected, in the sense that long-term investors prefer a more stable country (as results from the reserve requirement). In fact, FDI was predominant in Chile, whereas in Latin America as a whole it accounted for only one-fourth of total flows in the first half of the 1990s.[46] The flows, however, do not encompass the same money or the same investor; it is a different investor with a different behavior, closely connected to productive investment. On the one hand, FDI creates new capacity, which contributes to capital formation and also increases importation, in particular of capital goods. Given the size of the inflows, therefore, the foreign currency market experiences a smaller excess supply than in the case of financial inflows. On the other hand, FDI in Chile has behaved as a permanent variable, while other flows have acted

---

42. References to Chilean-style policy for dealing with capital flow instability are frequent in the main circles where these issues are discussed, for example, by people such as Andrew Crockett, Paul Krugman, Dani Rodrik, and Lawrence Summers. See, for example, Stiglitz (1998), then vice president of the World Bank; see also *El Diario*, Santiago, March 30, 2000, which quotes Horst Koehler, the recently appointed managing director of the IMF.

43. De Gregorio, Edwards, and Valdés (2000); Edwards (1999b); Le Fort and Lehman (2000); Schmidt-Hebbel, Hernández, and Gallego (1999).

44. See, for instance, Rodrik and Velasco (1999); Tapia (2000).

45. De Gregorio, Edwards, and Valdés (2000); Edwards, (1999b); Valdés-Prieto and Soto (1998).

46. It should be pointed out that loans associated with FDI remained subject to the reserve requirement. Since the average maturity of these loans was around seven years, the cost incidence was small, while it did minimize the risk that short-term loans would be disguised as long-term flows.

as transitory disturbances.[47] Because FDI is much less volatile than other types of incoming capital, macroeconomic regulatory policies such as reserve requirements that are based on short-term or volatile inflows will encourage long-term stability over continued volatility.

Some observers have stated that the effectiveness of measures to discourage capital inflows is only temporary, since private sector agents generally find ways around such measures.[48] In principle, a number of loopholes facilitate such evasion. One is to underbill imports or overbill exports. Another is to delay payment for imports or accelerate export receipts. A third possibility is to bring in funds through the informal currency market. Fourth, short-term funds can be registered as FDI, although this was a costly option since Chilean law required FDI to remain in the country for at least a year. Nonetheless, this method was becoming an important loophole, so the authorities agreed to eliminate it. Fifth, business partners may arrange back-to-back operations in which, for instance, one party pays for imports with a local bank deposit in Chilean pesos rather than foreign currency, while the exporter is then paid in foreign currency through a bank in his or her country. All of these tactics (and others) are possible, but they all imply costs, and some may have undesirable repercussions on the tax liabilities of those employing them to circumvent reserve requirements. Though a certain level of evasion is inevitable, there is no evidence suggesting large-scale evasion of measures to discourage short-term capital, as shown by the reserve deposits actually made and the collection of the equivalent fee by the Central Bank.

The most recent studies tend to confirm that the reserve requirement also reduced total inflows and moderated exchange rate appreciation.[49] Qualitative analysis reinforces the conclusion: Chile confronted a supply of foreign funds that was greater (in relation to its GDP) than other Latin American countries, owing to its more attractive economic performance and its greater political stability in the early 1990s. Nevertheless, exchange rate appreciation and the current account deficit (as a fraction of GDP or exports) were smaller, on average, than in the other countries in the region that received large amounts of foreign capital.[50]

All of these studies coincide in their assessment that the reserve requirements maintained an adequate spread between domestic and inter-

47. Agosin and Ffrench-Davis (2001); Le Fort and Lehmann (2000).
48. See, for example, Valdés-Prieto and Soto (1998).
49. Le Fort and Lehmann (2000); Schmidt-Hebbel, Hernández, and Gallego (1999).
50. See Ffrench-Davis (2000, chap. 10).

national interest rates and thus provided room for monetary policy. This factor was important in the process of sustained growth seen throughout the decade, since frequent mini-adjustments by the Central Bank prevented the need for maxi-adjustments and allowed the economy to remain persistently at or near its productive capacity or production frontier. Actual output thus coincided with potential output. The resulting perception of real sustainable stability stimulated capital formation and the growth of productive capacity and employment.[51]

The combination of policies used involved financial costs for the monetary authority, since accumulation of large volumes of foreign currency implies a significant cost. This also generates a social cost for the economy, since the profitability of these assets abroad is naturally less than interest payments on the Central Bank liabilities issued to sterilize the monetary effects of accumulating reserves. The losses for the Central Bank are estimated at 0.5 percent of GDP annually. Evidence shows that disincentives to short-term, liquid capital inflows tended to reduce the magnitude of the financial costs of sterilization and generated substantial macroeconomic benefits. Even more flexible and timely management of the intensity and coverage of the reserve requirement and additional mechanisms by the monetary authority would undoubtedly have kept the financial costs lower.[52] Furthermore, the existence of high levels of reserves has frequently been a very important stabilizing factor in emerging economies facing crisis situations, as was proved in Chile in the next episode.

Domestic Strengths and External Vulnerability: 1996–97

The previous section examined how prudential policy in the first half of the 1990s was effective in achieving objectives of macroeconomic sustainability during a capital surge. In 1995, the year in which the tequila crisis erupted, GDP dropped in Mexico and Argentina by 6.1 percent and 3 percent, respectively, whereas output rose 10 percent in Chile in a great show of external strength (helped by a positive terms-of-trade shock).[53] Paradoxically, satisfactory performance was one of the causes of the disequilibria

51. Agosin (1998); Ffrench-Davis and Reisen (1998).
52. Another potential source of real compensation for the Central Bank losses is the exchange rate band, which allows the exchange rate board to buy cheap (near the floor) and to sell expensive (near the top). This would generate profits only if there is not an excessively strong revaluation of the band.
53. A negative impact was felt only on the stock market. See Ffrench-Davis (2000, chap. 10).

built in 1996–97. In the first place, foreign investors' confidence in the strength of the Chilean economy encouraged them to invest massively, which created additional pressure on the exchange rate and tested the economy's capacity for efficient absorption. Second, a generalized optimism characterized the world financial environment, based on the notion that the international community had been learning how to handle international crises and that virulent crises were gone forever. One reflection of this was the attempt by the IMF, at its annual meeting in Hong Kong in October 1997, to achieve a mandate to promote capital account liberalization among member countries. Lobbying pressure and a strong fashion toward financial liberalization were enormous factors that were well received in Chile, where many actors felt themselves immune from the effects of financial crises. Third, some officials understandably let themselves be swayed by this euphoric atmosphere, accepting as sustainable a rising external deficit and the sharp appreciation of the real exchange rate.

Chile thus gave in to the pressures of the dominant international and domestic environment at the time. It indeed managed to reduce inflation quickly, but it paid a price in the form of the imbalances this generated.[54] The general policy was kept in place, against the fashion, but the authorities failed to strengthen measures in the face of the very abundant supply of capital during 1996–97. The combination of policies and the intensity with which they were applied remained constant. The surge clearly weakened the fundamentals of the Chilean economy: the current account deficit rose, the exchange rate appreciated, and the stock of liquid foreign liabilities grew somewhat. The deterioration certainly could have been checked during the boom by means of higher reserve requirements and other measures. Nevertheless, a notorious complacency reigned while the new boom made the country increasingly vulnerable to external shocks.

The effects of contagion from the Asian crisis began in late 1997 and were felt strongly in 1998–99. This time, Chile experienced a sharp drop in the terms of trade, equivalent to 3 percent of GDP per year. At the same time, the large 1996–97 capital inflows gave way to outflows of domestic and foreign funds, and the nominal exchange rate began to depreciate. This correction process interrupted the most successful period of economic growth recorded in Chile's history, which lasted from 1991 to 1998.

54. An overwhelming proportion of operators pushed for greater deregulation and maintained that larger external deficits were sustainable. Following the crisis, most of them blamed what they called excessive fiscal spending as the source of the subsequent recessive adjustment. This hypothesis has no empirical support, however, as shown below.

The New Wave of Capital

As shown in figure 3-2 above, the tequila crisis led to a considerable reduction in net capital inflows to Chile. This is mostly explained by the behavior of portfolio flows, which entirely disappeared in Chile, as in the rest
of Latin America. Despite the reduction in the most volatile flows, the confidence of long-term investors was striking, as reflected in increased FDI.

Capital flows returned to the region shortly after the tequila crisis. Net
inflows to Latin America grew from U.S.$30 billion in 1995 to U.S.$80
billion in 1997. Of this, a larger share than in the preceding years went to
Chile. The image of a successful country on solid footing attracted foreign
investors in massive quantities. In 1997, net inflows climbed to more than
10 percent of GDP.

The foreign capital boom of 1996–97 involved some changes in composition. FDI remained high. Portfolio flows increased sharply, however,
despite the fact that these were subject to the reserve requirement. The
progressive increase of investment abroad, which started at the beginning
of the decade, reached considerable levels. Some of this investment was increasingly funded by borrowing abroad. At the same time, the main institutional investors—the private pension funds—had placed only slightly
over 0.5 percent of their assets abroad by mid-1997.

In 1998, for the third time in sixteen years, financial flows to Latin
America underwent a drastic reversal and actually became negative. The
crisis was ameliorated by the presence of FDI, however. In 1982, most of
the loans were bank loans with variable interest rates. This time, the bulk
of flows were from FDI, which tends to be a more friendly component in
periods of crisis, and these remained high in Chile. The behavior of FDI
also tends to be anticyclical, reducing the amount of profit that can be sent
abroad. In fact, FDI remittances fell from U.S.$1.9 billion in 1997 to
U.S.$1.1 billion in 1999.

Investment abroad intensified even more. Devaluatory expectations
(starting in late 1997) triggered a massive exit of funds through those open
channels. Pension fund outflows, for example, increased notably starting
in late 1997, when expectations shifted from appreciation to depreciation.
Outflows from January 1998 to June 1999 peaked at the equivalent of 4.8
percent of 1998 GDP, or 12 percent of the funds.[55] The 10 percent drop

55. A hurried financial deregulation runs the risk of leaving too many exit doors open, which can
be a massive oversight when the market is nervous and expectations are shifting to the devaluatory side
(as was duly advised in Ffrench-Davis, Agosin, and Uthoff, 1995). This tends to make it more diffi-

in aggregate demand, and the recession it generated, were partly associated with the monetary contraction resulting from additional devaluating pressures caused by these outflows.

Policy after the Success of 1995

The set of policies available to authorities in the second half of the 1990s was relatively unchanged, including responsible surplus-based budget management. However, the use of such tools had strongly different features compared with the previous episode, and the economic approach thus constituted a different variety of policy. In particular, authorities demonstrated a marked passivity at the time that the imbalances were generated, and their highly risky nature was underestimated. A proof is that the target for a sustainable current account deficit was raised from 3.5 percent to 5 percent of GDP. This contrasts with the active management of the previous capital boom of 1991–94, and it highlights the fact that the survival of macroeconomic balances requires a highly pragmatic and prudent approach to episodes of financial euphoria.

As in the previous episodes, the cycle closed with negative external shocks. This time, the shock came from Asia and was very intense, but the breadth of its repercussions was closely linked to the Chilean economy's degree of exposure.

POLICIES FOR REGULATING CAPITAL INFLOWS   An examination of capital inflow regulation does not reveal significant changes, despite strong pressures by lobbyists pushing for full liberalization of the capital account. Not bending to those pressures deserves clear recognition, given the world environment of financial euphoria. The reserve requirement stayed at 30 percent with a one-year term for much of the period, with only minor adjustments.[56] Still, there was a radical shift in how the problem was approached. As analyzed above, the authorities made explicit efforts in the

---

cult to sustain exchange rate and macroeconomic stability, and it makes international financial crises more painful. Such was the case in Chile in 1998–99, when the pension funds and chapter XII investors were responsible for the capital flight that worsened the external imbalance. Curiously, analysts have practically ignored this highly significant fact.

56. In June 1996, the possibility of renewing a trade credit more than once a year was eliminated to close a loophole. A threshold (U.S.$200,000) under which small transactions were not subject to reserve requirements was set in December 1996 to help reduce the operating costs of the instrument. This exemption became a source of evasion, however, and then the threshold was lowered to U.S.$100,000 in March 1997.

first half of the 1990s to address the stability of key macroeconomic prices and not to create vulnerability to eventual external shocks; these efforts included limiting the growth of the current account deficit and restraining currency revaluation.[57] The external accounts and the exchange rate were monitored continuously, and there was ample willingness to refine the tools by increasing their coverage and evaluating their effects. The various instruments used were not ends in themselves, but only means to achieving the objectives mentioned.

The approach was rather different after the tequila crisis. Chile's strength in the tequila crisis sent a signal of invulnerability to many. The perception of Chile as solid and different from the rest of Latin America provoked doubt about the need to use the prudential macroeconomic instruments, which many analysts considered inefficient or unnecessary for a modern country. The result was a complacent attitude on the part of the authorities, who failed to prevent the development of evident imbalances in 1996–97, on account of the abundant inflows, and then took no measures to solve them when it was possible to do so, namely, during the boom. On the contrary, the prevailing trend was to "modernize" the management of the capital account and to take advantage of currency appreciation in the fight against inflation, as had been done two decades earlier.

As a part of the move toward financial integration, measures were taken to facilitate the investment of Chilean capital abroad. The percentage of foreign investment authorized to pension funds was raised from 6 percent in 1995 to 12 percent in April 1997, and new alternatives for such investment were opened up.[58] Rather than discouraging entry, the changes encouraged exit. This was supposed to diversify risk. Given the extremely optimistic expectations about the national economy and the opportunities for profit that the domestic markets offered in 1996–97, the outflows of funds were modest until expectations shifted to devaluation (see figure 3-3). While the changes did allow the funds to diversify risk as intended, they clearly increased risk for the economy as a whole, as demonstrated in 1998–99.

Throughout this period, the Central Bank did not dismantle policies. The government, for its part, forcefully defended the reserve requirement in negotiations of a free trade agreement with Canada. When the Asian crisis began to be strongly felt, portfolio and other short-term inflows plummeted. The Central Bank confronted this phase of the cycle, com-

57. See Ffrench-Davis, Agosin, and Uthoff (1995) for more detail.
58. The limit was raised to 16 percent in January 1999.

Figure 3-3. *Chilean Pension Fund Outflows and Real Exchange Rate*

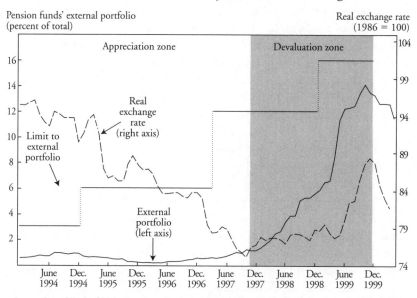

Source: Central Bank of Chile; Superintendencia de Administradoras de Fondos de Pensiones de Chile (SAFP).

bined with a depressed external capital supply, by lowering the reserve requirement to 10 percent in June 1998 and then to 0 percent in September. Authorities stated, however, that this was only a resetting of the parameters and that its use would continue to be relevant for confronting renewed capital surges.[59]

EXCHANGE RATE POLICY   The plentiful supply of capital flows after 1995 kept the exchange rate close to the floor of the band until the end of 1997. Given the overwhelming expectations of appreciation following the tequila shock, the large spread between the expected profitability of peso-denominated and dollar-denominated funds (along with a good outlook for large Chilean firms) offered foreign portfolio and short-term investors a potentially very lucrative opportunity despite the reserve requirement they paid to enter the domestic financial market.

Although the Central Bank formally adhered to a crawling band in 1996–97, the flexibility of the exchange rate was, in fact, increasing. Thus the Bank, as well as most observers, gradually moved toward one of the

59. Massad (2000).

two corner solutions that was increasingly in fashion: full foreign exchange flexibility. For instance, to lower the floor of the band (beyond a formal broadening of the band to ±12.5 percent in early 1997), authorities made contradictory adjustments in the weights assigned to the currency basket, causing a loss of credibility for the basket.[60] The external inflation used to calculate the referential exchange rate was overestimated, which generated considerable additional revaluation of 10 percentage points between 1995 and 1997. Furthermore, an annual 2 percent appreciation of the reference rate had been set in November 1995, based on the assumption that Chilean productivity would grow more rapidly than that of its main trading partners. At the same time, however, the Bank accumulated significant amounts of international reserves.

When exchange rate expectations shifted in Chile in late 1997, the Central Bank operated asymmetrically. It now strongly held back depreciating pressures by selling abundant reserves, thus preventing a correction of the exchange rate value. The authorities argued that accepting a sharp devaluation would be significantly inflationary in an economy operating on the productive frontier and with a high external deficit. In our view, an ambitious anti-inflationary objective was again predominant. In mid-1998, the band was drastically shortened right at the moment of greatest uncertainty, and the macroeconomic adjustment process was led by interest rate hikes; this intensified the monetary effects of outflows. The Central Bank was sending a signal that it would not give in to devaluatory pressures in the market. The band was widened again at the end of 1998 and then suspended in September 1999 to allow the exchange rate to adjust, now in the context of strongly depressed domestic absorption (see table 3-5).

The Consequences of a Prone-to-Risk Policy

Macroeconomic policy in 1996–97 proved unable to prevent the creation of imbalances in the external sector. As discussed above, the financial environment was characterized by an overoptimistic mood of success and invulnerability. Most participants seemingly ignored the danger of a financial crisis, which is always present in today's volatile world.

The economy took in large inflows in the form of FDI, which sur-

60. In November 1994, the weight of the dollar was reduced from 50 percent to 45 percent, reflecting the declining influence of that currency in Chile trade. It was arbitrarily raised to 80 percent in January 1997. For a comparative analysis of bands in Chile, Israel, and Mexico, see Helpman, Leiderman, and Bufman (1994). On Chile, Colombia, and Israel, see Williamson (1996).

Table 3-5. *Asian crisis in Chile, 1996-99*

Indicator	1996	1997	1998	1999
GDP[a]	7.4	7.4	3.9	−1.1
Aggregate expenditure[a]	7.9	9.1	3.9	−10.0
Fiscal expenditure[a]	9.6	6.1	6.3	5.7
Exports[a]	11.8	9.4	5.9	6.9
Imports[a]	11.8	12.9	5.4	−14.3
Current account deficit[b]	5.8	5.7	6.2	0.2
Real exchange rate[c]	84.7	78.2	78.0	82.4
Terms-of-trade effect[d]	−3.4	0.6	−3.0	0.2

Source: Based on data from the Central Bank of Chile; DIPRES (2000); Ffrench-Davis (2001).
a. Official figures at 1986 constant prices, annual growth (percent).
b. Current prices, percent of GDP.
c. Index, 1986 = 100.
d. Current prices, percent of GDP.

passed all previous records when they reached 6.8 percent of GDP in 1996–97. The signs of solvency and stability that Chile exhibited in the tequila crisis no doubt contributed to attracting these funds. The supply to emerging economies also underwent a significant positive shift that heightened the country-specific trend. At the same time, portfolio flows experienced unusual growth despite the cost of the reserve requirement. The evidence thus indicates that entry to the market was considered cheap in comparison with the very positive economic parameters and a strong likelihood that the real exchange rate would appreciate as a result of the large supply of foreign capital.[61] This is a classical case of an imbalance creating bubbles in the exchange rate market and in aggregate demand.

The Central Bank made heavy purchases of foreign currency, but it was unable to avoid a very significant real exchange rate appreciation (16 percent between the 1995 average and October 1997). The appreciation and the creation of liquidity by the inflows, in turn, sharply stimulated aggregate demand and biased it towards tradables. The current account deficit thus rose to 5.7 percent of GDP. Key macroeconomic prices had clearly become outliers, and instruments for dealing with excessive financial flows needed to be strengthened. The Central Bank, however, declared itself unable to fulfil its commitment to defending a more stable and com-

61. See Herrera and Valdés (1997). Country risk was again reduced; the *Euromoney* index, for instance, improved from 72.9 in 1995 to 79.0 in 1997.

petitive long-term exchange rate.[62] Instead, it gave priority to the inflationary goal, which was facilitated by the appreciating trend.

The situation called for a demand-reducing adjustment focused on the control of the external imbalance. Given that the large supply of capital inflows was the source of the disequilibrium, measures were needed to increase the cost of inflows, to devalue the real exchange rate, and not only to raise the cost of domestic credit (that is, the interest rate). The maintenance of a constant rate and coverage of the reserve requirement, without the implementation of additional measures, became insufficient for dealing with the massive capital inflow in 1996–97.[63] If the prudential regulation of inflows had been strengthened in 1996–97, it would have accomplished the triple goal of regulating the growth of the stock of liquid external liabilities, softening appreciation, and moderating the increase in aggregate expenditure.

A controversial issue involves the level of fiscal responsibility for the excess aggregate demand of 1996–97. An expansionary fiscal policy was recorded in the period, with government expenditure rising somewhat faster than GDP (7.9 versus 7.4 percent a year). However, several points have to be taken into account to fairly assess this fact. First, the fiscal expenditure with macroeconomic effects represents only one-fifth of the economy. The large majority of the pulls behind the 8.5 percent growth in domestic aggregate demand in the period were in the private sector, which accounted for 90 percent of the expenditure increase. A fiscal contribution to moderating total expenditure would thus have been insufficient. Second, the main components in the increased fiscal expenditure were education, justice, and infrastructure. All three areas underwent major and widely demanded transformations, with a political consensus around increasing expenditure on them. Third, the fiscal budget showed a surplus over 2 percent GDP and, consequently, overfinanced its expenditure. Moreover, the government stopped borrowing from the World Bank and the Inter-American Development Bank (IDB) and prepaid debt. Fourth, the measured fiscal surplus does not include resources accumulated in the Copper Buffer Fund.

Here again, imbalances were externally generated and overwhelmingly private. The government's responsibility in this case lay in its failure to

---

62. See, for example, the president of the Central Bank's statements in the Chilean business newspaper *Estrategia,* October 16, 1997.

63. Le Fort and Lehmann (2000, p. 33) offer a similar assessment. Le Fort was at that time the director of the Central Bank's International Division.

enforce coordination between the Central Bank and the Ministry of Finance.[64] This shortcoming was related to the Central Bank's autonomy. Authorities need to recognized that there is not a single form of autonomy in the world, but rather several alternative ones.

As a result of the lack of timely and sufficiently strong measures, the Asian crisis found Chile with a significantly appreciated exchange rate, an overstimulated aggregate demand, and a high current account deficit that was double the 1990–95 average. This all added up to a level of vulnerability that was unprecedented in the decade, and Chile received a strong trade shock. Nevertheless, if the reserve requirement had not been maintained, portfolio inflows would have been much greater, the overall flow more significant, and the exchange rate appreciation more marked.[65]

Financial capital began to flow out in late 1997 and accelerated in 1998–99. The nominal exchange rate depreciated to correct for misalignment.[66] This time, the impact of the exit of foreign capital was aggravated by the outflows associated with pension funds, which intensified the devaluating pressures on the exchange rate. The channels that had been progressively opened up over the course of the decade, under the argument they would moderate the abundance of foreign currency in boom periods and diversify risk, were effectively used only during the bust. Thus the objective was not achieved during the boom. Rather, the mechanism caused a significant loss of international reserves during the crisis, a monetary contraction, and a sharpening of the recessionary adjustment in 1998–99.

The cumulative current account deficit was moderate during the decade thanks to the active management of inflows in the first half of the 1990s and the persistence of regulations in the following years with only gradual liberalization. The stock of foreign liabilities was relatively low, and volatile funds played only a minor role, creating external imbalances only in 1996 and 1997. These conditions, together with the country's considerable international reserves, put Chile on a better footing than in the

64. The lack of coordination between the Central Bank and the government was evident. As mentioned, the Central Bank authorities expressed no concern about imbalances in the external sector, while the Minister of Economics, for instance, held that "it is necessary to intensify and strengthen policies such as the reserve requirement to reduce exchange rate appreciation." *Estrategia*, September 26, 1997.

65. Schmidt-Hebbel, Hernández, and Gallego (1999); Le Fort and Lehmann (2000).

66. The real exchange rate reached its peak for 1999 in November. This depreciation represented a movement toward equilibrium, in correction of the disequilibrium of 1996–97. The real exchange rate actually recovered its 1995 average level; this real rate tended to prevail in the second semester of 2000, after strong swings during the first semester.

previous crises for confronting the hardships of trade and financial shock caused by the Asian recession. The domestic financial system did not suffer radically, as a result of the strictness of the Chilean banking commission. Nonperforming loans as a percentage of total loans rose from 0.97 percent in December 1997 to 1.8 percent at its worst moment in April 1999—a level comparable to 1992, a crisis-free year.[67] This is remarkable given that aggregate demand fell by 10 percent.

Still, the social and economic costs were significant. Production underutilization in 1999 fell by about U.S.$7 billion, opening a gap of approximately 10 percent between actual GDP and productive capacity that year. Together with the increase in interest rates, this gap caused gross fixed investment to fall 17 percent, jeopardizing the potential GDP growth of 7 percent on average. Unemployment exceeded 10 percent of the labor force in 1999–2000, which reversed some of the progress that had been made in reducing poverty and inequality since 1990.[68]

Concluding Remarks

The rich experience of Chilean policy in managing foreign capital surges throws light on key principles and specific instruments for exploiting the benefits and minimizing the costs of financial globalization. Despite the extent to which globalization reduces the space for action, there is still room for each country to foster its objectives. In this sense, a country that falls victim to a financial crisis of external origin is never blameless. We have solid evidence that market imbalances in the exchange rate, high current account deficits, and excessive shares of short-term or liquid funds make a small, open economy vulnerable in a crisis. The challenge, then, is to fight worsening in these parameters.

Exchange rate policy has proved to be one of the key elements in the development of recent crises in Chile. Freezing the exchange rate as part of a price stabilization policy in the late 1970s and keeping it frozen for three years entailed a very significant outlier real price of the dollar, based on an unsustainable level of capital inflows. The discrepancy stimulated and financed a high current account deficit up to 1981, and a correction was to be expected. When it occurred in 1982, the economic and social results

67. SBIF (2000).
68. See Ffrench-Davis (2001, chap. 9).

were very negative: GDP fell 17 percent, and the unemployment rate jumped to over 30 percent. In the 1990s, policy aimed at preventing a repeat performance. The use of a managed crawling band reduced exchange rate volatility while moderating its appreciation up to the mid-1990s. This supported the target of maintaining an exchange rate that was consistent with the export model, at the expense of the objective of reducing inflation more quickly. The approach was successful in the first-half of the 1990s.[69] After the tequila crisis, however, the Central Bank did not check the large appreciation. Monetary authorities gave precedence to achieving more ambitious inflation goals despite an increased current account deficit and an excessive aggregate demand, thus repeating risky behavior of the past.

A curious fact of the Chilean case is that the three financial boom episodes generated different outcomes with the consistent use of certain tools to regulate capital inflows, in particular, an unremunerated reserve requirement on short-term capital. The main lesson is that an instrument that alters relative prices in the market, as does the reserve requirement, cannot remain unchanged in the face of a changing supply of foreign funds. Furthermore, a policy of sustainable macroeconomic balances must not rest solely on one inflexible instrument, excellent though the instrument may be. A reserve requirement was clearly ineffective in saving the economy from the debt crisis in 1982, while in 1996–97 its impact was insufficient for staving off contagion from the Asian crisis. However, one might ask what would have happened if it had not been applied in those cases. Empirical evidence indicates that the imbalances would have been worse, especially with regard to the Asian crisis. The effectiveness of this sort of instrument depends, first, on the values set for its parameters and the degree of coverage, and, second, on complementary policies that support the strategy, as in the first half of the 1990s. These policies include fiscal responsibility and effective prudential supervision of the financial system.

Regulatory instruments such as a reserve requirement have costs.[70] Quasi-fiscal losses stemming from excessive accumulation of reserves and a lower GDP growth rate owing to higher interest rates are those most often mentioned. A serious assessment requires weighing these effects against their macroeconomic benefits. The benefits are extensive, deriving from

---

69. The economy's performance in that period was quite satisfactory, with dynamic exports and a gradual but large reduction of inflation. Sebastián Edwards summarizes this point well: "Given the relative success of the Chilean band system, it is surprising that more countries have not adopted this type of regime" (1999b, p. 37).

70. Schmidt-Hebbel, Hernández, and Gallego (1999) summarize and measure these costs.

the notable imperfections of international financial markets (including high volatility and information asymmetry). By helping to counterbalance these market imperfections, measures to drive capital flows at a sustainable level and moderate exchange rate instability reduce both the likelihood of a crisis and its potential costs. They are also associated with gains in growth because of their positive impact on resource allocation and export development. Finally, economic growth benefits enormously when monetary authorities are given room to regulate spending and smooth the cyclical behavior of the economy. These benefits are difficult to quantify, since the moderation of cyclical behavior not only creates a better environment for productive investment and growth, but also favors social development by improving conditions of poverty, income distribution, and welfare programs, a dimension which is highly sensitive to economic fluctuations.[71]

In liberalizing the capital account, a dose of prudence is also in order with regard to outflows. Observers and lobbyists argue that the funds are too big for Chile and that profitability is increased by investing abroad. Chile is a capital-scarce country, however, and the return of capital tends to be higher in Chile than in developed countries. Hence, it is questionable whether funds saved by Chileans and held by pension funds should be encouraged to move abroad rather than preferentially invested domestically. The issue is particularly controversial when macroeconomic risk diversification is achieved at the expense of macroeconomic sustainability because of its procyclical nature. This issue requires further discussion and analysis.

Another of the dimensions that make Chile an interesting case study is the development of its domestic financial institutional structures. The deregulation of banking activity in the absence of a proper framework of prudential regulation in the 1970s was, without a doubt, a destabilizing element that contributed to an overborrowing syndrome.[72] Moreover, progress made to address the weakness contributed to the development of one of the healthiest financial markets among emerging countries and fostered macroeconomic stability throughout the 1990s. It would be a mistake, however, to emphasize this dimension as the sole explanation of financial crisis in Chile. In the three episodes examined here, the domestic financial market operated as the channel for only a portion of the funds coming into the country. This was particularly relevant in the 1990s, when bank loans constituted a minority of inflows. As the events of 1998–99

71. See Rodrik (2001).
72. McKinnon and Pill (1997).

showed, the high quality of Chile's domestic financial market did not prevent the country from becoming quite vulnerable to external financial shocks. This point must be stressed, given the persistence of the dangerous hypothesis that efficient banking supervision is enough to impede the absorption of excessive inflows.

The fact that fiscal policy did not play a leading role in managing the Chilean crises may seem unusual, especially considering the broad literature that explains external sector crises as a result of unsustainable budget deficits. In the three Chilean episodes discussed here, however, the fiscal situation was solid, with surpluses each year.[73] Deficits were registered only in 1982 and 1999, and these were the result of the crisis conditions, not the cause. They were thus associated with external disequilibria during the previous booms. Once more, the lesson is not to trust in a single fundamental of the economy as adequate protection.

The challenge of making good use of foreign capital in emerging economies, ensuring the healthy domestic absorption of funds, and keeping vulnerability to external factors low requires a comprehensive set of measures. It is indispensable to take an active, pragmatic approach to checking the development of imbalances, to respond to shifts in domestic and external variables, to work in close coordination with a solidly structured financial sector, to implement a foreign exchange policy that prevents excessive misalignment of the real rate, to design fiscal and monetary policies that keep a handle on spending, and to take a flexible approach to managing the capital account so that measures taken are consistent with the realities of a developing country where capital is not only scarce in absolute terms but minuscule in comparison with the volume of capital that can flood a country through an imperfect and volatile international financial market. Chile's experience shows that all of this is possible and that the challenge is ongoing. New problems will always arise, and dangerous temptations can exact a heavy price tomorrow for today's success.

References

Agosin, M. R. 1998. "Capital Inflows and Investment Performance: Chile in the 1990s." In *Capital Flows and Investment Performance: Lessons from Latin America*, edited by R. Ffrench-Davis and H. Reisen. Paris: Organization for Economic Cooperation and Development (OECD), Development Center.

73. Larraín (1991); DIPRES (2000).

Agosin, M. R., and R. Ffrench-Davis. 2001. "Managing Capital Inflows in Chile." In *Short-Term Capital Flows and Economic Crises*, edited by S. Griffith-Jones, M. F. Montes, and A. Nasution. WIDER/Oxford University Press.

Aninat, E., and C. Larraín. 1996. "Flujos de capitales: lecciones a partir de la experiencia chilena." *Revista de la CEPAL* 60 (December).

Arellano, J. P., and R. Cortázar. 1982. "Del milagro a la crisis: algunas reflexiones sobre el momento económico." *Colección Estudios CIEPLAN* 8 (July).

Calderón, A., and S. Griffith-Jones. 1995. "Los nuevos flujos de capital extranjero en la economía chilena: acceso renovado y nuevos usos." *Serie Desarrollo Productivo* 24. Santiago: United Nations Economic Commission for Latin America and the Caribbean.

Calvo, G., L. Leiderman, and C. Reinhart. 1993. "Capital Inflows and Real Exchange Appreciation in Latin America: The Role of External Factors." *IMF Staff Papers* 40(1).

Cortázar, R., and J. Marshall. 1980. "Indice de precios al consumidor en Chile: 1970–78." *Colección Estudios CIEPLAN* 4 (November).

De Gregorio, J., S. Edwards, and R. Valdés. 2000. "Controls on Capital Inflows: Do They Work?" Working Paper 7645. Cambridge, Mass.: National Bureau of Economic Research.

Díaz-Alejandro, C. F. 1985. "Goodbye Financial Repression, Hello Financial Crash." *Journal of Development Economics* 19(1/2).

DIPRES (Dirección de Presupuestos del Ministerio de Hacienda). 2000. *Estadísticas de las finanzas públicas: 1990–1999*. Santiago.

Edwards, S. 1999a. "Capital Flows to Latin America." In *International Capital Flows*, edited by M. Feldstein. University of Chicago Press for the National Bureau of Economic Research.

———. 1999b. "How Effective Are Capital Controls?" *Journal of Economic Perspectives* 13(4): 65–84.

Edwards, S., and A. Cox Edwards. 1987. *Monetarism and Liberalization: The Chilean Experiment*. Cambridge, Mass.: Ballinger.

Ffrench-Davis, R. 1984. "International Private Lending and Borrowing Strategies of Developing Countries." *Journal of Development Planning* 14.

———. 2000. *Reforming the Reforms in Latin America: Macroeconomics, Trade, Finance*. Macmillan/Palgrave.

———. 2001. *Economic Reforms in Chile: From Dictatorship to Democracy*. University of Michigan Press.

Ffrench-Davis, R., M. R. Agosin, and A. Uthoff. 1995. "Capital Movements, Export Strategy and Macroeconomic Stability in Chile." In *Coping with Capital Surges. The Return of Finance to Latin America*, edited by R. Ffrench-Davis and S. Griffith-Jones. Lynne Rienner.

Ffrench-Davis, R., and J. P. Arellano. 1981. "Apertura financiera externa: la experiencia chilena en 1973–80." *Colección Estudios CIEPLAN* 5 (July).

Ffrench-Davis, R., and J. De Gregorio. 1987. "Orígenes y efectos del endeudamiento externo en Chile: antes y después de la crisis." *El Trimestre Económico* 213 and 214 (January-March). Mexico City.

Ffrench-Davis, R., and S. Griffith-Jones, eds. 1995. *Coping with Capital Surges. The Return of Finance to Latin America*. Lynne Rienner.

Ffrench-Davis, R., and H. Reisen, eds. 1998. *Capital Flows and Investment Performance: Lessons from Latin America.* Paris: Organization for Economic Cooperation and Development (OECD), Development Center.

Harberger, A. 1985. "Observations on the Chilean Economy, 1973–83." *Economic Development and Cultural Change* 33 (April).

Held, G., and F. Jiménez. 2001. "Liberalización, crisis y reforma del sistema financiero chileno." Ford Foundation.

Helpman, E., L. Leiderman, and G. Bufman. 1994. "A New Breed of Exchange Rate Bands: Chile, Israel and Mexico." *Economic Policy* 9(19).

Herrera, L. O., and R. Valdés. 1997. "Encaje y autonomía monetaria en Chile." Santiago: Central Bank of Chile. Unpublished.

Labán, R., and F. Larraín. 1997. "Can a Liberalization of Capital Outflows Increase Net Capital Inflows?" *Journal of International Money and Finance* 16(3): 415–31.

Larraín, C. 1995. "Internacionalización y supervisión de la banca en Chile." *Estudios Públicos* 60 (Spring). Santiago.

Larraín, F. 1991. "Public Sector Behavior in a Highly Indebted Country: The Contrasting Chilean Experience, 1970–85." In *The Public Sector and the Latin American Crisis,* edited by F. Larraín and M. Selowsky. San Francisco: ICS Press.

Le Fort, G., and S. Lehmann. 2000. "El encaje, los flujos de capitales y el gasto: una evaluación empírica." Working Paper 64. Santiago: Central Bank of Chile.

Massad, C. 2000. "Capital Flows in Chile: Changes and Policies in the Nineties." In *Financial Globalization and the Emerging Economies.* Santiago: United Nations Economic Commission for Latin America and the Caribbean (ECLAC) and Jacques Maritain International Institute.

McKinnon, R., and H. Pill. 1997. "Credible Economic Liberalization and Overborrowing." *American Economic Review* 87(2).

Mizala, A. 1992. "Las reformas económicas de los años setenta y la industria manufacturera." *Colección Estudios CIEPLAN* 35 (September).

Morandé, F. 1992. "The Dynamic of Real Asset Prices, the Real Exchange Rate, Trade Reforms and Foreign Capital Inflows: Chile, 1976–89." *Journal of Development Economics* 39(1):111–39.

Morandé, F., and K. Schmidt-Hebbel, eds. 1998. *Del auge a la crisis de 1982: ensayos sobre liberación financiera y endeudamiento en Chile.* Santiago: Instituto Interamericano de Mercados de Capital and Georgetown University/ILADES.

Reinstein A., and F. Rosende. 2000. "Reforma financiera en Chile." In *La transformación económica de Chile,* edited by F. Larraín and R. Vergara. Santiago: CEP.

Rodrik, D.2001. "Why Is There So Much Economic Insecurity in Latin America?" *CEPAL Review* 73 (April).

Rodrik, D., and A. Velasco. 1999. "Short-Term Capital Flows." Working Paper 7364. Cambridge, Mass.: National Bureau of Economic Research.

Sanhueza, G. 1999. "La crisis financiera en los años ochenta en Chile: análisis de sus soluciones y su costo." *Economía Chilena* 2(1). Santiago: Central Bank of Chile.

SBIF (Superintendencia de Bancos e Instituciones Financieras de Chile). 2000. "Evolución de la banca en el tercer trimestre de 2000." Santiago. Mimeographed.

Schmidt-Hebbel, K., L. Hernández, and F. Gallego. 1999. "Capital Controls in Chile: Effective? Efficient?" Working Paper 59. Santiago: Central Bank of Chile.

Stiglitz, J. 1998. "The Role of the Financial System in Development." Paper Prepared for the Fourth Annual Bank Conference on Development in Latin America and the Caribbean, San Salvador. World Bank (June).

Tapia, D. 1979. "Apertura al mercado financiero internacional." In *Institucionalidad económica e integración financiera con el exterior*. Santiago: Instituto de Estudios Bancarios.

Tapia, H. 2000. "Liquidez de los capitales externos y probabilidad de crisis." Unpublished.

Valdés-Prieto, S. 1992. "Financial Liberalization and the Capital Account: Chile, 1974–84." In *Financial Reform: Theory and Experience*, edited by E. Caprio and J. Hanson. Cambridge University Press.

Valdés-Prieto, S., and M. Soto. 1998. "New Selective Capital Controls in Chile: Are They Effective?" *Empirica* 25(2).

Williamson, J. 1992. "Acerca de la liberalización de la cuenta de capitales." *Estudios de Economía* 19(2). Santiago: Universidad de Chile.

———. 1996. *The Crawling Band as an Exchange Rate Regime: Lessons from Israel, Chile, and Colombia*. Washington: Institute for International Economics (IIE).

Zahler, R. 1980. "Repercusiones monetarias y reales de la apertura financiera: el caso chileno, 1975–78." *Revista de la CEPAL* 10 (April).

———. 1998. "El Banco Central y la política macroeconómica de Chile en los años noventa." *Revista de la CEPAL* 64 (April).

JAIME ROS*

4 From the Capital Surge to the Financial Crisis and Beyond: The Mexican Economy in the 1990s

In the early 1990s, after almost a decade of economic decline and high inflation, the Mexican economy appeared to be on its way to recovering economic growth and price stability. Privatization revenues and a Brady agreement had facilitated a large reduction in domestic and external public debt, and a successful stabilization program was expected to finally allow the economy to take advantage of the structural reforms undertaken since the mid-1980s. Or so it appeared to the many observers who believed that Mexico, a model reformer and successful emerging market, was to become a Latin American economic miracle. Optimistic expectations became even more widespread when the North American Free Trade Agreement (NAFTA) was approved in 1993. The optimistic view was further reinforced by the fact that the Mexican government had complemented wide-ranging economic reforms with an anti-poverty program aimed at meeting the country's pressing needs in health and education infrastructure. To many, then, Mexico appeared to be on a firm path toward economic and social modernization.

By the end of 1994, however, the Mexican economy was in a financial crisis and entering its worst recession since the Great Depression of the

*I am grateful to Maiju Perala for research assistance and to Ricardo Ffrench-Davis and participants at seminars held at the United Nations Economic Commission for Latin America and the Caribbean (ECLAC) in Santiago, Chile, for helpful comments.

1930s. The Mexican government was unable to roll over its debt following the December devaluation of the peso. Amid surging fears of default, an unprecedented international rescue package was implemented in early 1995 to stop panic selling of Mexican debt. The country also experienced political turmoil and violence throughout 1994: an armed uprising by the Zapatistas in January (on the day NAFTA came into effect), the assassination of the presidential candidate in March and of the Secretary General of the Partido Revolucionario Institutional (PRI) in September, and the resignation in November of the Assistant Attorney General who had been in charge of investigating the latter assassination.

The country was considered one of the most successful emerging markets, and it was supposed to be entering a period of sustained prosperity, yet in the mid-1990s it became immersed in the worst economic crisis of the last seventy years. How could the Mexican government find itself on the brink of default just four years after the first Brady agreement, despite having significantly reduced its external and domestic debt? These are the issues addressed in this paper. The following section reviews the episode of massive capital inflows of the early 1990s and discusses the financial reforms that preceded it. The paper then examines how the success of the Mexican economy in attracting foreign capital itself undermined the fundamentals of the economy by causing a large appreciation of the peso, a misallocation of resources, and increasing financial fragility. The next section analyzes how these three consequences of the capital surge combined and interacted to produce the crash landing that was to follow, and compares our interpretation to other explanations of the crisis. The final section looks at the performance of the economy after the crisis and discusses its medium-term prospects.

Financial Liberalization, Debt Reduction, and the Capital Surge

While the capital surge of the early 1990s extended to most countries in Latin America and other developing regions, Mexico had a prominent place in this episode: nearly half of the capital inflows to Latin America in the period 1990–93 went to Mexico (see table 4-1). These massive inflows had their origin in a diversity of circumstances: almost all of the various internal and external determinants of capital movements had a positive effect on inflows. The external environment was characterized by the con-

Table 4-1. *Capital Inflows in Mexico and Latin America, 1977–95*
Billions of dollars, except as indicated

Capital inflows	1977–81	1983–89	1990–93	1994–95
Total annual capital inflows (net)				
Latin America	28.86	8.15	45.89	38.55
Mexico	8.15	−0.66	22.50	3.60
Mexico as percent of total	28.3	−8.1	49.0	9.3
Foreign direct investment				
Latin America	n.a.	n.a.	11.43	17.28
Mexico	n.a.	n.a.	4.05	6.99
Mexico as percent of total	n.a.	n.a.	35.4	40.4
Other capital inflows (net)				
Latin America	n.a.	n.a.	34.46	21.27
Mexico	n.a.	n.a.	18.45	−3.39
Mexico as percent of total	n.a.	n.a.	53.5	−15.9

Source: United Nations Economic Commission for Latin America and the Caribbean (ECLAC),
América Latina y el Caribe: políticas para mejorar la inserción en la economía mundial, 2d ed.,
Santiago: Fondo de Cultura Económica and ECLAC, 1998, tables 9.1 and 9.4.

tinuous reduction of foreign interest rates through early 1994, a U.S. recession in the early 1990s, and regulatory changes introduced by the U.S. Securities Exchange Commission, all of which were favorable to an increase in U.S. investment abroad.[1] In addition, improved terms of trade in the late 1980s and the debt relief agreement with creditor banks led to a reduction in Mexico's risk premium.[2]

The favorable domestic factors arose out of the new institutional environment that characterized the Mexican economy as a result of the structural reforms initiated in the mid-1980s. The reforms that were most directly relevant to the capital surge include the liberalization of domestic financial markets and their opening to foreign investors, as well as the deregulation of foreign direct investments (FDI). Starting in 1988, a succes-

1. The regulatory changes—regulation S and rule 144A—stimulated portfolio investment in developing countries through the issue of American depository receipts (ADRs) on the New York stock market and the development of country funds in U.S. financial markets. See ECLAC (1995, 1998); Ffrench-Davis (2000, chap. 5). See also Banco de Mexico, *Informe Anual, 1993*, available at www. banixco.org.mx.

2. The Brady Plan was announced in March 1989 and an agreement in principle was signed in July 1989. Mexico became the first country to sign a debt agreement with commercial banks under the United States-sponsored plan in February 1990.

sion of measures relaxed reserve requirements, credit quotas to high priority sectors, and controls on interest rates; unified the controlled and free
exchange rates; and abolished the exchange controls that were adopted
during the 1982 crisis. Restrictions on foreign investments in the domestic bond and stock markets were eliminated in 1989 and 1990.[3] Throughout the 1980s, the De La Madrid and Salinas de Gortari administrations
liberally interpreted the Foreign Investment Law of 1973 and adopted a
series of regulatory changes to facilitate the inflow of FDI. These changes
culminated with a new Foreign Investment Law in 1993. The new Law
opened areas that had previously been closed to foreign companies and
eliminated the clause that restricted foreign participation in local firms to
49 percent. Other relevant policy changes include the privatization of the
banking system and telecommunications in 1991–92. In addition to dem-
onstrating the government's commitment to market-oriented reforms, privatization provided the government with large revenues that were used to
sharply reduce the burden of domestic and external debt in the fiscal accounts (see table 4-2).

These domestic reforms and positive external shocks, together with the
initiation of NAFTA negotiations in 1990, contributed to the surge of capital inflows through three channels. The first was a sharp reduction in the
country's risk premium—the improved image of Mexico as a good place to
invest. The debt relief agreement, the fall in foreign interest rates, and the
use of large privatization revenues to repay external debt in 1991–92 produced a substantial reduction of interest payments both as a percent of exports and as a percent of gross domestic product (GDP) (see table 4-3).
These indicators, which are conventionally used by national and foreign investors to evaluate country risk, fell in the 1990s to levels below those
achieved in the mid-1970s before the onset of the balance-of-payments crisis that was under gestation in the period 1974–76.[4] Moreover, privatization revenues also financed a sharp reduction of domestic, as well as
external, government debt. By the first quarter of 1993, domestic debt was
down to half its real value in mid-1990. Total government debt had therefore fallen from 55 percent of GDP in 1990 to 35 percent in 1993, which

3. A decree in May 1989 liberalized the neutral-investment regime to promote the entry of foreign
investors into the local stock market. By late 1990, restrictions on the foreign purchase of domestic
bonds (largely government bonds) had been eliminated.

4. From 1990 to 1993, Mexico's foreign debt was upgraded by foreign risk evaluators, and in the
case of two Mexican development banks, it was given an investment grade rating (see Gurría, 1995).
This occurred despite the emergence of the first symptoms of serious financial vulnerability, as discussed below.

Table 4-2. *Mexico: Use of Privatization Revenues, 1991–92*

Destination of revenues	Percent of GDP		Billions of dollars			Percent of total
	1991	1992	1991	1992	1991–92	1991–92
Total revenues from privatization[a]	3.3	3.3	9.42	10.74	20.16	100
Financial deficit[b]	1.4	0.1	4.02	0.28	4.30	21.3
Net reduction of debt	1.9	3.2	5.39	10.46	15.85	78.6
External	1.5	0.8	4.39	2.55	6.94	34.4
Central Bank	1.9	0.2	5.49	0.70	6.19	30.7
Private sector total[c]	−1.6	2.2	−4.48	7.21	2.73	13.5
Residents[d]	1.8	1.5	5.03	4.94	9.97	49.5
Nonresidents[e]	−1.2	−2.7	−3.54	−8.77	−12.31	−61.1
Commercial banks	−2.1	3.4	−5.97	11.04	5.07	25.1

Source: J. Ros, "Mercados financieros y flujos de capital en México," in *Los capitales externos en las economías latinoamericanas,* edited by J. A. Ocampo, Bogotá: Fedesarrollo and Inter-American Development Bank (IDB), 1994. Calculations based on data from Banco de México, *Informe Anual,* 1991 and 1992, available at www.banixco.org.mx.

a. Includes cash revenues (or amortization of the banking privatization bonds) and reduction of the domestic or external public sector debt as a result of the reclassification of Mexican telecommunications as a private enterprise.

b. Accrued public financial deficit. Includes the accrued nonpaid interests that are only incorporated to the financial deficit at the time of liquidation.

c. Banking and nonbanking (includes nonresidents).

d. Nonbanking. Obtained as a residual of private sector debt reduction.

e. Foreign portfolio inflows to the money market (displayed with a negative sign).

is about half the average for the member countries of the Organization for Economic Cooperation and Development (OECD) and less than a third of that for Italy or Belgium.

A second channel was the opening of domestic financial markets, which had the same effect as a shift in the portfolio preferences of foreign investors between domestic and foreign assets. In an earlier study of the determinants of capital inflows, I find that the opening of the bond market accounts for most of the shift in asset preferences during the period.[5] Only after 1994— the year NAFTA went into effect and a year after Congress approved the new Foreign Investment Law—did FDI become significantly more important than in the 1960s and 1970s. This partly accounts for the heavy concentration of capital inflows in portfolio investments through late 1993.

The third channel, which interacted with the reduction in the risk premium, was the real appreciation of the peso and the very high interest rates

5. Ros (1994b).

Table 4-3. *Mexico: Macroeconomic Performance Indicators, 1988–98*
Percent

Indicator	1988	1989	1990	1991	1992	1993	1994	1995	1996	1997	1998
GDP growth	1.2	4.2	5.1	4.2	3.6	2.0	4.4	-6.2	5.2	6.7	4.8
Inflation	51.7	19.7	29.9	18.8	11.9	8.0	7.1	52.0	27.7	15.7	18.6
Real exchange rate (index)	100.0	94.6	89.9	82.0	75.0	70.8	73.6	106.6	96.7	85.5	86.4
Real interest rate[a]	7.3	13.8	1.0	-1.3	3.4	14.0	13.3	6.6	9.2	8.8	10.1
Private savings rate[b]	17.5	14.8	13.2	10.6	10.5	11.6	11.4	15.8	16.7		
Domestic savings rate[b]	21.4	19.5	20.3	19.0	18.1	18.2	18.0	18.5	22.5[c]	24.1[c]	20.5
Fixed private investment[b]	11.7	11.8	12.8	14.1	15.6	14.8	14.3	11.0	13.2	15.3	16.8
Fixed public investment[b]	3.9	4.0	4.2	4.1	3.8	3.8	4.9	3.6	2.9	3.0	2.5
Urban unemployment	3.6	3.0	2.8	2.6	2.8	3.4	3.7	6.2	5.5	3.8	3.2
Average real wage (index)	100.0	105.9	107.4	114.2	122.8	130.6	136.9	118.8	109.1	112.5	115.5
Trade[b]											
Exports	13.9	14.0	14.1	14.2	14.4	15.2	17.2	23.9	26.8	27.9	29.2
Imports	11.7	13.2	15.0	16.6	19.2	19.2	22.3	20.2	23.6	27.1	29.5
Capital account[b]											
Direct investment	1.6	1.5	1.1	1.8	1.6	1.5	3.5	3.1	2.9	3.7	2.9
Portfolio inflows	0.5	0.2	1.4	4.9	6.6	10.1	2.6	-3.2	4.2	1.5	0.4
Loans	-1.8	0.4	4.7	3.1	-0.6	1.0	0.4	7.5	-3.8	-2.6	1.1
Debt[b]											
Gross external debt	43.7	36.6	32.1	30.1	28.4	27.5	27.1	31.0	30.8	26.9	24.9
Gross domestic debt	22.4	23.4	20.9	16.8	11.8	10.2	10.8	9.5	6.8	7.4	8.9

Public finance[b]

Total expenditure	36.4	30.6	27.5	23.9	22.2	22.5	23.1	23.0	23.3	23.7	21.5
Operating expenditure	12.5	11.2	10.5	9.9	8.8	9.1	8.9	8.2	8.1	8.3	7.2
Investment	2.9	2.4	2.7	2.9	2.7	2.5	3.0	2.5	2.9	2.5	1.8
Domestic interest payments	12.5	9.0	6.8	3.1	2.2	1.5	1.1	2.6	2.3	2.5	1.5
External interest payments	3.6	3.3	2.3	1.9	1.5	1.2	1.2	2.0	2.1	1.6	1.4
Other	4.9	4.7	5.2	6.1	7.0	8.2	8.9	7.7	7.9	8.8	9.6
Total revenue	27.7	25.8	25.3	23.5	23.7	23.1	22.8	22.8	23.2	23.0	20.3
Federal government (total)	16.3	16.4	15.9	15.5	16.0	15.5	15.2	15.3	15.7	15.8	14.1
Taxes	11.4	11.1	10.7	10.7	11.3	11.4	11.3	9.3	9.0	9.8	10.4
Nontax federal revenue	5.0	5.3	5.2	4.8	4.8	4.1	3.9	6.0	6.7	6.0	3.7
Income shares											
Profits and interest[d]	56.5	56.0	54.5	52.9	51.8	50.4	49.8	54.6	55.9	n.a.	n.a.
Tradable goods sectors	25.1	21.3	19.1	17.5	16.0	14.2	13.8	17.0	19.2	n.a.	n.a.
Nontradable goods sectors	31.4	34.7	35.4	35.4	35.8	36.2	36.0	37.6	36.7	n.a.	n.a.
Skilled labor[e]	9.8	11.7	12.3	14.0	15.6	17.2	18.2	16.6	15.5	n.a.	n.a.
Other[f]	33.8	32.3	33.2	33.0	32.6	32.4	31.9	28.7	28.6	n.a.	n.a.

Source: Instituto Nacional de Estadística Geografía e Informática (INEGI), *National Accounts*, Indicators of Competitivity, various years; Banco de México, *Economic Information*; Organization for Economic Cooperation and Development (OECD), *OECD Economic Surveys*, various years; Secretaría de Hacienda y Crédito Público de México, historical data; International Monetary Fund (IMF), *International Financial Statistics*, various years; United Nations Economic Commission for Latin America and the Caribbean (ECLAC), *Economic Survey of Latin America and the Caribbean, 1998–99*.

a. Discontinuous series: 1988–92 calculations based on ECLAC data; 1993–98 calculations based on IMF statistics.

b. Percent of GDP.

c. Value not comparable with earlier series.

d. Operating surplus (excluding oil, agriculture, commerce, and other services) minus property income paid abroad plus government interest payments to the private sector.

e. Estimated using the average wage in construction as an upper limit to the wage of unskilled labor.

f. Unskilled labor and self-employed earnings. Estimated as a residual.

that prevailed during the initial stages of the disinflation program of late 1987. The annual real interest rate on three-month Treasury bills (CETES) in mid-1989 was still on the order of 19 percent to compensate for the inflation uncertainty that accompanied the disinflation process. The rapid success of the counterinflation program, which required a significant appreciation of the peso in real terms, implied extremely high ex post dollar interest rates on short-term domestic securities.

The magnitude and composition of the inflows were key elements for the macroeconomic consequences of the capital surge. Gross inflows increased tenfold from U.S.$3.5 billion in 1989 to U.S.$33.3 billion in 1993, before falling sharply in 1994.[6] Net inflows rose from negligible numbers to 12.6 percent of GDP at their peak in 1993. During the capital surge, the inflows were strongly biased toward highly liquid assets. The composition of these short-term investments changed over time. In the initial stages of the surge (1989 and 1990), inflows involved foreign loans to the private sector and the acquisition of bank deposits, but the liberalization of the domestic money and stock markets redirected inflows toward government bonds and stocks. Throughout the period, portfolio investments in the stock market increased rapidly and represented the largest component at the peak of the surge in 1993. From the end of 1990 to the end of 1993, the market value of the accumulated portfolio investments in the stock market jumped from U.S.$4.5 billion to U.S.$54.6 billion. In 1993 alone, the flow of portfolio investments in the stock market amounted to U.S.$28.4 billion.[7] Short-term outflows were dominant during the contraction after 1994: average portfolio investments fell to around 1.7 percent of GDP from 1994 to 1998, well below FDI (3.3 percent of GDP on average and about 20 percent of private domestic investment).

The cycle of capital movements appears to be especially marked in the case of Mexico, which has a history of being the main beneficiary of inflows during booms and the most vulnerable country during contractions. During periods of expanding capital inflows, the Mexican economy has tended to absorb a large share of the portfolio inflows into Latin America, much larger than its fraction of the less volatile FDI flows. This concentration of inflows in liquid assets increases Mexico's financial fragility relative to other countries, such that the downturn catches Mexico in a very vulnerable position. The result is that the country is generally one of the most severely hit by the reversal of the portfolio inflows and receives a very small share dur-

6. Banco de Mexico, *Informe Anual, 1994*, available at www.banixco.org.mx.
7. See Gurría (1995).

ing the period of contraction. The recent past has been an exception to this pattern. Financial turbulence started in East Asia and later in Russia and Brazil, while Mexico maintained a relatively solid position.

How Success Undermined the Fundamentals

The magnitude and composition of capital inflows should have raised three legitimate sources of concern for economic policy: the continuous appreciation of the peso in the midst of a rather radical trade liberalization process; an allocation of resources biased toward consumption rather than investment and toward the production of nontradables, which originated in the difficulties of adequately intermediating such massive inflows and resulted in slow economic expansion; and the increasing financial fragility that resulted from the concentration of inflows in highly liquid assets and the progressive deterioration of the banks balance sheets. This section discusses these three consequences of the capital surge.

Capital Inflows, Financial Markets, and the Real Appreciation of the Peso

The capital surge episode featured a large real appreciation of the peso: from 1988 to 1993, the real value of the peso increased by more than 40 percent (the real exchange rate fell by 30 percent; see table 4-3). The process of appreciation appears to have been even more dramatic if measured by the ratio of tradable to nontradable goods prices: the ratio fell from 140.9 in 1988 to 74.3 in 1993 (Gurría, 1995).[8] This section presents a formal analysis of the mechanisms at work behind the real appreciation and of the macroeconomic adjustment problem it generated. The analytical framework is based on a model of the goods and financial markets in which the exchange rate and the interest rate have a dual role, as key prices in the allocation of resources and as prices of financial assets.[9] First, they

8. In 1981, in the eve of the 1982 currency devaluations, the ratio was 98.1.

9. The model draws on Branson (1985), with elements borrowed from Ros (1994b, 1995a) and Ros and Skott (1998). It differs from Branson in two major areas. First, relative prices respond asymmetrically to excess demand and supply. While an increase in the demand for nontraded goods leads to a real appreciation of the currency (an increase in the relative price of nontraded goods), an excess supply leads to a downward output adjustment (leaving the real exchange rate, at least temporarily, at its initial level). Second, the model attributes an important role to changes in the position of the marginal investor in explaining the behavior of asset prices.

Figure 4-1. *Financial and Goods Markets*

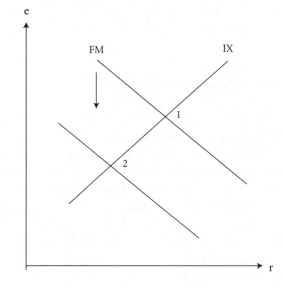

clear the goods market, that is, they guarantee the flow equilibrium of the economy, through their effects on desired investment, savings, and net exports. Second, they ensure financial equilibrium—the stock equilibrium of the economy—through their role as prices of financial assets.

Figure 4-1 shows the flow and stock equilibria of the economy at the intersection of two curves (the IX and FM curves in Branson's terminology).[10] The first curve (IX) is a locus of real exchange rate and real interest rate combinations along which desired investment is equal to savings (national plus foreign). Investment depends positively on the real exchange rate (on account of its positive effects on profitability) and inversely on the real interest rate. Given total employment, this locus is one along which the nontraded goods market clears through changes in the real exchange rate. It therefore has a positive slope in figure 4-1: a fall in the interest rate raises investment and creates excess demand for goods; the relative price of nontraded goods increases to clear the market for nontraded goods. Moving along the curve, lower values of the real exchange rate cause the current account deficit to increase, as the fall in the real exchange rate (appreciation of the domestic currency) leads to a larger gap between the demand for and domestic supply of traded goods.

10. See the appendix for a full exposition of the model.

The second curve (FM) is a locus of financial market equilibrium. In portfolio balance, the interest rate differential between domestic and foreign short-term securities, adjusted for exchange rate expectations, is equal to the risk premium on domestic securities. This premium is assumed to be a function of an exogenous component reflecting investors' subjective perceptions of country risk and the stock of external liabilities. With regressive expectations about the real exchange rate (see appendix), the locus slopes downward. An appreciation of the domestic currency tends to generate expectations of depreciation, which requires an increase in the domestic interest rate to maintain financial market equilibrium.

Consider now the situation in mid-1989. The current account deficit was on the order of 2.6 percent of GDP (roughly the average of the past three decades), and the real exchange rate was at its 1978 value (the average of the 1970–94 period). There were no significant expectations of real depreciation, and a high risk premium accounted for the large real interest rate differential between domestic and foreign securities.[11] Let these conditions be described by point 1 in figure 4-1. Starting with the debt relief agreement and the beginning of NAFTA negotiations in mid-1990, a series of positive shocks disturbed the initial stock equilibrium. These shocks reduced both the real interest rate and the real exchange rate; they also reduced the risk premium and shifted the FM curve down and to the left. As the FM curve shifts downward, the short-term equilibrium value of the domestic currency appreciates along the IX curve. The anticipation by financial markets of a fall in interest rates (and thus in the real exchange rate), as a result of the downward shifts in the FM curve, generates short-term expectations of real appreciation. Falling interest rates, real appreciation of the peso, and continuous expectations of real appreciation were indeed key features of Mexico's financial markets from mid-1990 to mid-1992.[12]

By mid-1992 the process of reducing domestic and external government liabilities ended, and the FM curve stopped shifting down. Exchange rate expectations then came to be dominated by the increased gap between

11. See Ros (1994b). The expected rate of real depreciation is obtained from the interest rate differential between CETES and the dollar-indexed Tesobonos and from the inflation expectations implicit in the differential between CETES and indexed Ajustabonos. Because the differential between Ajustabonos and CETES includes an inflation-uncertainty premium, the risk premium also reflects an inflation-uncertainty premium. Uncertainty about inflation was large in 1989, since the heterodox stabilization program launched in December 1987 had yet to prove its success. This contributed to the high measured risk premium between domestic and foreign securities.

12. Ros (1994b).

the exchange rate and its expected long term value.[13] At this point, the real interest rate would have to increase again to compensate for expectations of depreciation, which is what happened between the second and third quarters of 1992 when the expected rate of depreciation turned from negative to positive.

Subsequently, however, real interest rates remained surprisingly stable and low (until the political shocks of 1994), and the persistent gap between the current and long term real exchange rates failed to be reflected in higher interest rates. This appears to have been the consequence of a change in the position of the marginal investor (at the margin between domestic and foreign short term securities), as the stock of domestic government bonds changed hands between the bearish domestic wealth holders and the bullish foreign investors.[14]

Adjustments in the Goods and Labor Markets

Consider now the evolution of the goods and labor markets. The stylized facts here are, first, the rapid and unprecedented contraction of manufacturing employment and the expansion of underemployment in commerce and agriculture. These trends are shown in table 4-4, together with output and productivity performance during the crisis and post-crisis periods (1993–97). As shown in the table, the reduction in manufacturing employment is the result of a very high growth rate of labor productivity (6.0 percent per year) in the face of a rather slow rate of output growth (4.2 percent per year).

Second, wage inequality in the labor market increased in the early 1990s. Figure 4-2 shows the decline since 1988 in the relative labor earnings of the low wage sectors (namely, agriculture, construction, commerce, and services). Wage inequality also increased within sectors as the wage premium for skilled labor rose. Figure 4-3 illustrates the rising trend of white-collar wages relative to blue-collar wages in all manufacturing industries, while table 4-3 (above) tracks the redistribution between skilled and unskilled labor earnings that took place from 1988 to 1994. Other evidence reported in a number of studies similarly documents the increase in wage dispersion and shows that it largely revolved around the increase in skilled

13. Formally, this is equivalent to an upward shift in the FM curve.
14. Bulls and bears are defined here according to their perceptions about the future of the exchange rate. See Ros (1994b); Ibarra (1997).

Table 4-4. *Mexico: Output, Employment, and Productivity Growth, 1988–97*

Average annual growth rates

	Employment growth		Output growth		Productivity growth	
Sector	1988–93	1994–97	1988–93	1994–97	1988–93	1994–97
Total	3.1	3.2	3.7	2.4	0.6	−0.8
Mining[a]	−7.4	8.8	2.0	4.1	9.4	4.7
Manufacturing	−1.8	4.9	4.2	4.7	6.0	−0.2
Agriculture	5.8	0.5	1.9	1.7	−3.9	1.2
Nontradable goods	3.6[c]	3.9[c]	3.1	1.8	−0.5	−2.1
Construction	4.1	−1.7	4.9	0.1	0.8	1.8
Transport and communication	5.0	2.7	4.1	5.0	−0.9	2.3
Commerce[b]	5.1	3.4	4.3	1.0	−0.8	−2.4
Services	3.0	5.5[d]	3.9	1.6[d]	0.9	−3.9
Government	0.8	n.a.	0.9	n.a.	0.1	n.a.

Source: INEGI, *National Accounts*, various years; INEGI, *National Survey of Employment*, 1997.
a. Includes electricity.
b. Includes restaurants and hotels.
c. Includes unspecified activities.
d. Includes government.

relative to unskilled labor incomes.[15] As a result of these trends, the Gini coefficient of wage inequality increased from 0.46 in 1989 to 0.49 in 1992, and then to 0.53 in 1994.[16] The increase in wage inequality is, in turn, the single major factor behind the worsening of income distribution during the period.[17]

These stylized facts can be explained as consequences of trade liberalization and the real overvaluation of the peso, which caused intensified competition from imports and thus accelerated the rate of technology adoption and reduced the demand for low skilled workers in manufacturing. This hypothesis can be elaborated in the framework of a two-sector model (tradables and nontradables) in which tradable goods are produced under imperfect competition with unskilled labor as the variable factor, while skilled labor is largely fixed in the short run, since it is complementary to physical capital. Trade liberalization implied greater competition in

15. See Hanson and Harrison (1995); Cragg and Epelbaum (1996); Alarcón and McKinley (1997).
16. Lustig and Székely (1998), based on income and expenditure household surveys.
17. Ros and Lustig (1999).

Figure 4-2. *Mexico: Relative Labor Earnings in Low Wage Sectors,*
1988–97

Relative wage[a]

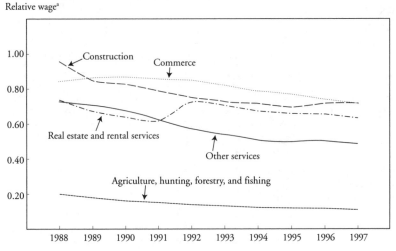

Source: INEGI, *Cuentas Nacionales.*
a. Average labor earnings in the sector relative to the ecomomy's average.

Figure 4-3. *Mexico: Ratio of White- to Blue-Collar Earnings in*
Manufacturing, 1988–97

Wage ratio

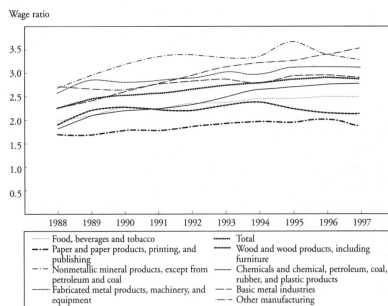

Source: INEGI, *Cuentas Nacionales.*

the domestic market and increased the share of imports in domestic demand. At the same time, the real value of the peso rose as a result of the capital inflows, the increased demand for nontradables, and the chosen exchange rate policy. Increased competition and the appreciation of the real currency, in turn, caused the profit markup over marginal costs in the import-competing goods sectors to fall. The profit squeeze is shown in table 4-3: the property income share fell continuously from 1988 to 1994, with a cumulative decline of 7 percentage points. The impact of the profit squeeze was very different among sectors, with a large redistribution taking place from the tradables toward the nontradables sectors. The lower profit markup had a negative effect on unskilled employment, since this is the variable factor that firms can adjust in the short run. This resulted in the tendency to substitute skilled for unskilled labor, which is observable in the industrial employment data.

Figure 4-4 shows the determination of the real wage (W/P) and the level of employment in the import-competing goods sector at the intersection of two schedules. The NN locus is the equilibrium schedule in the markets for unskilled labor and nontradables (which are intensive in unskilled labor). The schedule slopes upward: an increase in employment in the import-competing goods sector (L_T) reduces the labor supply to the nontradable goods sector and increases the real wage. The TT locus is the equilibrium schedule in the market for import-competing goods. It is downward sloping, since an increase in wages increases costs and prices in this sector, which reduces the demand for import-competing goods (to the benefit of imported and nontradable goods).

The increase in capital inflows generated an expansion in the demand for nontradable goods, which shifted the NN curve up and to the left. This increased the real wage and crowded out employment in the tradables sector. At the same time, the effects of trade liberalization and currency overvaluation on the goods and labor markets operated through three channels. First, the relative price of imported goods fell, shifting the TT locus down and to the left. Output demand and employment in the import-competing goods sector fell in the short run. Given nominal wages in the import-competing goods sector, the adjustment involved an expansion of employment in the nontradables sector, which reduced productivity and wages in that sector. This opened a gap between the wages of unskilled labor employed in the two sectors, observable in the increasing wage inequality between low- and high-wage sectors (see figure 4-2). The downward pressure on real wages in the import-competing goods sector eventually reduced the prod-

Figure 4-4. *Financial Flows, Exchange Rate, Wages, and Employment*

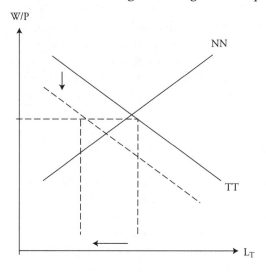

uct wage of unskilled labor there and generated an intrasectoral increase in the wage premium of skilled labor. The cost and relative price reductions in the import-competing goods sector tended to reestablish the initial relative prices, shifting the TT schedule upward. Even if the initial relative prices are reestablished in the long run, however, the displacement of local production by imports may have hysteresis effects which lead to a permanent increase of the ratio of imports to domestically produced import-competing goods. Through this second channel, the downward shift of the TT schedule may be permanent and has long-lasting effects on employment and real wages in the import-competing and nontradable goods sectors. These hysteresis effects are the consequence of the real currency appreciation associated with trade liberalization.

Finally, the intensified competition in the local market led to an increase in the price elasticity of demand facing producers of import-competing goods. The higher price elasticity reduced the firms' profit margins, which had two consequences. First, it implied a fall in the price of import-competing goods relative to nontradables and imported goods. This increased the demand for import-competing goods and shifted the TT schedule upward. Second, the fall in profitability tended to reduce investments in the import-competing goods sector and had negative longer-run effects on employment. This second effect—together with the short-run and long-run effects of import penetration discussed above—clearly dominated in the Mexican experience.

Currency overvaluation also had adverse effects on aggregate investment, to the extent that the increased profitability of nontradables was less than the reduced profitability of tradables. (As shown in table 4-3, the overall share of profits in total income fell.) Together with the distributive effect of the profit squeeze against incomes with relatively high savings rates, these adverse effects on investment explain why the rapid expansion of bank credit that accompanied the capital surge fuelled a consumption boom. From 1988 to 1994, the gap between private investment and savings increased by 6.2 percentage points of GDP. The increase was fully explained by a collapse of private savings (6.1 percentage points of GDP) rather than by any significant change in the investment rate.

The positive shock that hit the Mexican economy in the early 1990s reduced the real interest rate and appreciated the real value of the domestic currency. In figure 4-1 (above), as the real value of the peso appreciates along the IX curve, the current account deficit increases. Thus a large current account deficit emerges at point 2 in the figure, exacerbated by the effects of the capital surge on domestic private savings. From then on, the resulting accumulation of foreign liabilities should produce an upward pressure on the domestic savings rate (or a reduction in the domestic investment rate or both), while the expectations of depreciation should generate an increase in the real interest rate. The resulting excess supply of nontradable goods would, in a flex price economy, tend to increase the price ratio of tradable to nontradable goods and to gradually correct the current account deficit. The IX line shifts up in this process, bringing about a real depreciation. Because expectations of depreciation fall as the gap between the current and the long-term exchange rate closes, the path also features a reduction of domestic interest rates.

This mechanism of current account correction and resource reallocation will fail to operate if the excess supply of goods does not lead to a lower relative price of nontradables. In that case, the ex ante excess of savings over investment will turn into a downward output adjustment. This output adjustment can be seen as a downward shift of the IX curve that prevents the correction of the real exchange rate, the fall of depreciation expectations, and the reduction of the interest rate. Currency overvaluation persists, and large current account deficits remain in the face of a deceleration of growth.

Such was the actual path followed by the Mexican economy: growth

Figure 4-5. *Mexico: Trade Balance and GDP Growth, 1970–99*

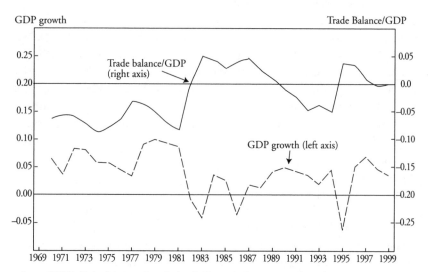

Source: INEGI, *National Accounts;* Organization for Economic Cooperation and Development, *OECD Economic Surveys,* various years.

slowed in 1992 and substantially decelerated in 1993. As shown in figure 4-5, the decline in the trade balance occurred in the midst of sluggish growth and then persisted with excess capacity. While earlier current account deficits on the order of 7–8 percent were an exceptional feature occurring only in periods of very fast economic expansion (with GDP growth rates above 7 percent), in the early 1990s these large deficits appeared in a semistagnant economy and showed no signs of reversal as growth decelerated in 1992 and 1993.[18]

Financial Fragility and the Deterioration of the Banks' Balance Sheets

In the financial markets, the continuous accumulation of external liabilities eventually caused the FM curve to shift up, putting further upward pressure on the interest rate (at a given value of the real exchange rate, as the IX curve endogenously shifted down with the level of output). As already discussed, this increase in interest rates was initially prevented by the foreign purchase of the stock of government bonds held by local investors. In 1994, three additional processes came into play to hold down

18. For a full discussion, see Ros (1994b) and Lustig and Ros (1998).

Figure 4-6. *Mexican Government Short-Term Public Debt*

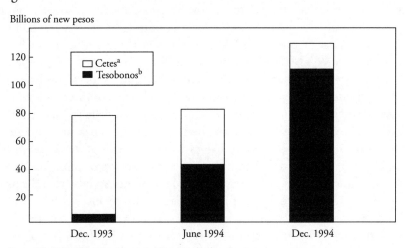

Billions of new pesos

Source: World Bank, based on Banco de México, *Indicadores Económicos*.
a. Three-month peso-denominated Treasury bonds.
b. Three-month dollar-indexed bonds.

the government debt service. All three were the consequence of the slow-down of capital inflows that occurred as foreign investors, who had become the major holders of short-term government securities by late 1993, became increasingly fearful about the government's ability to hold to its exchange rate policy.

The first process, which began in full in early 1994 and accelerated with the assassination of the PRI's presidential candidate in March of that year, was the dollarization of the stock of domestic government debt. As peso-denominated Treasury bills (CETES) fell due, they were converted into dollar-indexed short-term bonds (Tesobonos) (see figure 4-6). This process represented a change in the position of the investor at the margin between CETES and Tesobonos, and it prevented even larger increases in the CETES rate.

The second process was the shortening of the average maturity of government bonds. The dollarization of debt involved not only peso-denominated short-term Treasury bills, but also peso-denominated securities with longer maturities. These long-term bonds (Bondes and inflation-adjusted Ajustabonos) were similarly converted into Tesobonos (which is why in figure 4-6 the stock of Tesobonos in December is larger than the stock of CETES a year earlier). The result was a steady decline in the average maturity of the debt from a peak of 306 days in April 1994 to 206 days in December 1994. A consequence of this process was the large amount of debt coming due in 1995 in the form of both CETES and Tesobonos. In the case of Tesobonos, U.S.$28.6 billion was due in 1995, of which 35 percent (U.S.$9.9 billion) was due in the first quarter.[19]

The third process involved the Central Bank's decision to sterilize the effects of reserve losses on the money supply. The loss of international reserves stemmed from massive speculative attacks, especially in March 1994 at the time of the Colosio assassination, as well as from a more gradual process that occurred the second half of 1994 as a result of the persistently large current account deficit in the face of the slowdown of capital inflows. The sterilization of reserve losses prevented the money supply from shrinking and contributed to keeping interest rates relatively low.

Why did the government choose this course of action, given the high risks involved? The next section addresses this question fully, but part of the answer has to do with another set of problems created by the capital surge: the increased vulnerability of a recently privatized banking system. A large fraction of capital inflows was intermediated by commercial banks, whether directly through bank deposits acquired by foreigners or indirectly through the substitution, in the portfolio of residents, of commercial bank liabilities for financial assets sold to foreigners. Trigueros estimates that domestic banks decided the final destination of close to 60 percent of foreign inflows.[20] As a result of the intermediation of capital inflows, commercial bank credit to the nonfinancial private sector multiplied by a factor of 3.5 between the end of 1989 and the end of 1994.

Credit was misallocated, partly as the unavoidable result of the magnitude of its expansion, partly in response to the profit squeeze on investment, and partly because the demand for consumer durables had been repressed for almost a decade. The result was an imbalance between the financing of consumption and the financing of investment, together with a deterioration in the banks' balance sheets. The magnitude of the imbalance in the financing of consumption and investment is revealed in the fact that household credit increased from 9.6 percent of total credit in December of 1989 to 26.7 percent in November 1994. The deterioration of the banks' balance sheets is revealed by the increase in nonperforming loans, which rose from a negligible amount in 1990 to about 9 percent of

19. See Cole and Kehoe (1996); Ibarra (1997).
20. Trigueros (1998).

total bank loans in 1994. At the same time, dollar-denominated bank liabilities expanded rapidly: dollar deposits (mostly in commercial banks) captured nearly one-fourth of total capital inflows from the beginning of 1990 to the third quarter of 1994. This expansion, together with the fact that the sources of foreign exchange necessary to service the commercial bank liabilities in hard currency were not being created, created a vulnerability to exchange rate changes that had dramatic consequences after the December 1994 devaluation.

The Crisis: Currency, Banking or Debt?

The path that the economy had taken well before the convulsions of 1994 was likely to lead, sooner or later, to a slowdown of capital inflows. The slowdown came in 1994, and it partly took the form of a series of speculative attacks associated with the political shocks of that year. The government was then faced essentially with three options: an early (albeit already overdue) exchange rate realignment through a shift to a floating rate, a step devaluation, or a faster slide of the band ceiling; a monetary contraction resulting from unsterilized reserve losses, which would have led to large increases in interest rates; or an expansion of domestic credit to sterilize the effects of reserve losses on the monetary base, combined with the dollarization of domestic debt to stem capital flight and prevent further increases in interest rates.

The first option was probably judged unnecessary and likely to send the wrong signal concerning the Central Bank's commitment to price stability (which had recently been elevated to the sole objective of the Central Bank). The second option was discarded, probably out of the fear on the part of the Central Bank that such a monetary contraction would trigger a major banking crisis. The possibility of a major banking crisis was undoubtedly a real reason for concern: the speculative attack in March had caused a loss of one-third of international reserves, and the balance sheet of the banking system had deteriorated as a result of the earlier overexpansion of bank credit.

Another major reason why the authorities pursued the third option was that they assumed the slowdown in capital inflows was temporary and reversible. The slowdown was not seen as the beginning of a macroeconomic adjustment process that required a change in exchange rate policy in order to proceed more or less smoothly. Policymakers—and for a while many financial market participants—wrongly assessed the deterioration of the real fundamentals of the Mexican economy that began well before the political events and hard policy dilemmas of 1994. They thus perceived the reserve losses following the runs on the peso in January and March as unique events that had unfortunately, but only temporarily, sent a healthy situation off course. Furthermore, the sterilization and debt management decisions temporarily accomplished their intended objectives of stopping capital flight and relieving the pressure on domestic interest rates. Domestic interest rates started to fall in July, and from April to mid-November there were no new dramatic drops in international reserves. Reserves did undergo a gradual and continuous loss, however, as the slowdown in capital inflows persisted and the large current account deficit was financed by running down reserves.

The Currency Crisis

Interpretations of the Mexican crisis fall into several categories. A first distinction can be made between a disequilibrium view, which emphasizes the economy's real disequilibria (that is, real overvaluation and unsustainable current account deficit), and an equilibrium speculative attack view, which gives preeminence to the excessive monetary growth that caused reserves to decline until the exchange rate regime collapsed.[21] The interpretation presented here clearly falls into the real disequilibria school. The current account deficit was indeed on an unsustainable path, and its correction would eventually require a large real exchange rate realignment. Between 1989 and 1993, the current account deficit (excluding interest on the debt) averaged 31.7 percent of exports. Given an export growth rate of 8.7 per-

---

21. See Sachs, Velasco, and Tornell (1996) for this distinction. Within the first view, Dornbusch and Werner (1994) explain the real appreciation of the peso as the result of the exchange rate–based stabilization program in the face of sluggish price adjustments; Ros (1994b, 1995a) and Lustig and Ros (1998) discuss the so-called Mexican disease, that is, the unsustainability of exchange rate and trade policies and the misallocation effects of the capital surge, which led to the collapse of private savings and unsustainable current account deficits; and Atkeson and Ríos-Rull (1996) argue that Mexico hit a borrowing constraint in early 1994 following the collapse of domestic savings in previous years. For examples of the second view, which emphasizes the inconsistency between exchange rate and monetary policy generated by the Central Bank's attempt to sterilize the reserve losses arising from the slowdown of capital inflows, see Sachs, Velasco, and Tornell (1995) and Calvo and Mendoza (1996). The standard speculative attack model is Krugman (1979); later generations of speculative attack models are discussed below. Many of these interpretations go beyond the events leading to the devaluation in December 1994, encompassing the post-devaluation crisis. Here, the focus is on their interpretations of the economic mechanisms that led to the devaluation.

cent per year (the average for 1989–93), Dadush, Dhareshwar, and Johannes estimate a steady-state ratio of foreign liabilities to exports of 3.6.[22] I reach similar conclusions in earlier papers.[23] The World Bank debt tables classify a country as severely indebted if its debt is greater than 220 percent of exports, that is, well below the 3.6 steady state ratio in Mexico. It is thus unlikely that foreign investors would have been willing to finance this high debt path. The Mexican economy would therefore have faced severe debt and balance-of-payments problems well before reaching the steady state.[24]

The presence of real disequilibria, however, is not enough to explain the currency crisis, let alone its timing. What if, for example, the Central Bank had chosen not to finance the current account deficit by running down reserves during most of 1994? Before looking more closely at this question, a further distinction must be made among three different types of currency crisis models, this time within the speculative attack hypothesis.[25] Fundamentalist or first-generation models á la Krugman or Flood and Garber are based on the inconsistency between an exchange rate peg and an expansionary monetary and fiscal policy.[26] When forced to monetize a fiscal deficit, the central bank defends the peg by gradually losing reserves. The inconsistency is perceived by speculators, and it consequently leads to a speculative attack and the collapse of the exchange rate. These are fundamentalist models in the sense that the origin of the crisis has to do with wrong fundamentals, in this case the inconsistency between the rate of domestic credit expansion and the exchange rate regime.

Second-generation models endogenize economic policy by introducing the costs and benefits of devaluation. Speculative attacks can then arise in the absence of any fundamental problems.[27] The reason is that the endogeneity of economic policy introduces an element of indeterminacy and self-fulfilling prophecy: a government may be willing to continue to defend the exchange rate (and follow a consistent monetary policy) if no speculative attacks occur, but it would rather shift to a floating regime if a speculative at-

22. Dadush, Dhareshwar, and Johannes (1994).

23. Ros (1994a, 1994b).

24. The 3.6 ratio of foreign liabilities to exports includes not only debt, but also other forms of foreign investments. This qualification does little, however, to reduce the assessment of Mexico's vulnerability, given that most of these investments took the form of highly liquid and volatile portfolio inflows with a rate of return that was usually higher than that of foreign debt.

25. See P. Krugman, *Balance Sheets, the Transfer Problem and Financial Crises*, 1999, available at web.mit.edu/krugman/www/.

26. Krugman (1979); Flood and Garber (1984).

27. Obstfeld (1986).

tack forces it to face the alternative of monetary contraction. The private
sector is in equilibrium in both cases, and multiple equilibria exist within a
range of costs and benefits of defending the exchange rate. Self-fulfilling
changes in expectations can then shift the economy from one equilibrium to
the other. The European Monetary System (EMS) currency crises of 1992,
it has been argued, fit into this framework.[28] Sachs, Tornell, and Velasco
apply a variant of the argument to the 1994 Mexican devaluation (see
below).[29]

Finally, the Asian crises inspired third-generation models that emphasize banking problems and the effect of moral hazard on lending and investments.[30] Calvo and Mendoza bring elements of this approach into
their interpretation of the Mexican crisis.[31]

Although these elements are not entirely absent from the Mexican crisis, none of these views fits the Mexican experience especially well. The
inconsistency between exchange rate policy and a monetary policy that
sterilized reserve losses, for example, was certainly a feature of economic
policy in 1994, but the reserve losses were the result of the speculative attacks themselves rather than, as in the Krugman model, of a fiscal deficit
financed by the Central Bank's expansion of credit which then led to a speculative attack. Trying to understand the crisis through such a model leaves
unexplained the very phenomenon that these first-generation models aim
to explain (namely, the speculative attack). The more gradual reserve losses
during the second half of the year, which resulted from the slowdown of
capital inflows in the face of a huge current account deficit, were validated
by the sterilization policies followed throughout the year. Here again, however, first-generation models cannot explain why the Central Bank followed this course of action: there was no fiscal deficit to account for the
expansion of domestic credit.

Why, then, did the Central Bank validate the reserve losses instead of
adopting a tight monetary policy to reduce the current account deficit and
increase the capital account surplus? Such a tight monetary policy probably would not have prevented new speculative attacks and the eventual
collapse of the exchange rate, even over a short horizon. The reasons that
the Central Bank pursued the policy it did are related to the second- and

28. Obstfeld (1994).

29. Sachs, Tornell, and Velasco (1996).

30. See P. Krugman, *Balance Sheets, the Transfer Problem and Financial Crises*, 1999, available at
web.mit.edu/krugman/www/.

31. Calvo and Mendoza (1996).

third-generation models, though in rather subtle ways. First, as argued earlier, the Central Bank had to consider the prospect of a severe banking crisis. Banking problems thus had an important role in the developments leading to the devaluation, as in recent models inspired by the Asian crisis. This factor, however, did not arise because the currency crisis was a by-product of a bank run caused by perceptions of insolvency or even because government guarantees and moral hazard generated bad lending and a hidden fiscal deficit. Banking problems were important because the fragility of the banking system, which resulted from the nature of the capital surge, influenced the authorities' decision to sterilize the reserve losses and dollarize the domestic debt.

Second, a contractionary monetary policy would have generated additional high costs. The fact that the exchange rate regime was eventually abandoned reveals a growing conflict between exchange rate stability and other objectives of economic policy, including employment and growth. The costs of not devaluing, as perceived by the government, eventually became too high. Ibarra applies this reasoning to explain why the exchange rate policy was abandoned just after the change in administration in December 1994, when the costs of devaluing (such as the loss of reputation) could be minimized.[32] Moreover, the adoption of a tight monetary policy would have lacked credibility in the eyes of investors, given the high costs involved. High interest rates are often the prelude to speculative attacks precisely because they signal to speculators the high costs of defending the peg.

The endogeneity of economic policy, as emphasized by second-generation models of currency crises, was thus clearly relevant to the Mexican experience. This does not mean, however, that the endogeneity of economic policy necessarily generated multiple equilibria, as argued by Sachs, Tornell, and Velasco.[33] They hold that multiple equilibria arise when a sufficiently high (but not too high) level of government debt generates partial credibility in the exchange rate peg. The government's incentive to devalue then depends on self-fulfilling expectations of devaluation: if these are low, interest rates allow debt to continue to be serviced without devaluing; if they are high, they create a strong incentive for the government to reduce the value of the debt through devaluation. The interdependence between exchange rate policy and devaluation expectations opens the door to self-fulfilling outcomes.

32. Ibarra (1997).
33. Sachs, Tornell, and Velasco (1996).

This argument has two unsatisfactory features. First, devaluation could hardly inflate away the real value of the debt, which by this time was mostly in dollars or dollar-indexed bonds. It is doubtful, then, that this could have acted as an incentive to devalue, so the incentives for the government action on December 20 have to be found elsewhere. Second, the argument neglects the effects that the change in government probably had on the net costs of devaluing. As argued by Ibarra, the reduction in these costs—as perceived by a new administration that could blame the previous government for the necessary policy change—was probably a major factor in the timing of the devaluation.[34] If this is the case, as I believe it is, a model with multiple equilibria is not necessary for explaining the currency crisis. The shift in the perceived costs of devaluing probably moved the economy from a situation in which the peg had enough credibility that a single equilibrium existed (because nobody believed that the old administration would devalue on the eve of the change in government) to one in which a commitment by the new government to pursue the same exchange rate policy had so little credibility, given the costs of maintaining the policy, that again a single equilibrium (devaluation) existed.

All this suggests that a hybrid model—in which worsening policy trade-offs and shifting perceptions of the costs of devaluation interact against the background of real disequilibria, a large current account deficit, and a slowdown in capital inflows—is perhaps the most useful approach for understanding the timing of the devaluation of December 1994. In this view, the presence of banking problems, together with policymakers' confidence about the future course of capital inflows, decisively influenced the monetary and debt management decisions of 1994. The strategy of dollarizing debt to avoid tightening monetary policy had run its course, with practically the whole stock of CETES existing in late 1993 converted into Tesobonos by December 1994, and capital inflows had not recovered sufficiently. In this context, the change in administration that took place in December abruptly modified the perceived costs of devaluing.

The Debt Crisis

So far the paper has focused on the policy actions and events leading to the devaluation. Understanding the currency crisis, however, is only half of the story, for the Mexican crisis involved more than the exchange rate.

---

34. Ibarra (1997).

Multiple equilibria arguments become much more relevant in understanding the second half of the story than they were in the first.

After November 1991, the peso-dollar parity fluctuated within a band based on a fixed floor and a sliding ceiling (with a daily crawling peg of 0.04 centavos after October 1992). The peso depreciated within the band by around 10 percent in 1994, and the band's ceiling was raised 15 percent on December 20, 1994. The announcement of the new band ceiling immediately sent the value of the dollar to the new 4 peso ceiling, and it is estimated that U.S.$5 billion left the country in the course of two days. The Central Bank then decided to withdraw from the foreign exchange market. A rapid and substantial depreciation followed: the dollar parity went from 4 pesos on December 20 to 6.35 on January 30 and 7.55 on March 9, when an emergency economic program for 1995 finally stopped the slide. Panic selling of government debt sent the risk premium on Tesobonos (measured as the interest rate differential between Tesobonos and U.S. Treasury bills) from less than two percentage points before the devaluation to five percentage points at the end of December and twenty percentage points at the end of January 1995.[35] On December 27, a Tesobono refinancing auction was cancelled because investors were no longer willing to hold these obligations at interest rates acceptable to the Mexican authorities. In the stock market, it is likely that some of the investors who had their funds invested in pesos interpreted the devaluation as a breach of contract. Their reaction was to withdraw their capital as soon as possible. Toward the second week of January, Mexico was on the verge of default, and the financial markets of Latin America and other regions increasingly began to be affected.

In sum, the collapse of the peso rapidly degenerated into a debt crisis. Why was a government that had substantially reduced its foreign and domestic liabilities since 1990 unable to roll over its debt in December 1994 and January 1995? Why was a rescue package of about U.S.$50 billion eventually required to stop the collapse of the peso? The answer to these questions is that fears of default surged in the face of the small level of reserves left at the Central Bank at the time of floating and the large amount of short-term debt, particularly dollar-linked Tesobonos, coming due throughout 1995. Moreover, the dollarization of the debt meant that devaluation did nothing to reduce the high ratio of Tesobonos to reserves, while it increased the real value of the dollar debt in pesos. Through sim-

35. Cole and Kehoe (1996); Ibarra (1997).

ple arithmetic calculations, investors saw that payments coming due in 1995 (which were estimated at about U.S.$50 billion, assuming that most of the short-term debt would not be rolled over) were far greater than the estimated resources available: international reserves in the Bank of Mexico were about U.S.$6 billion. Individual investors may have been willing to roll over their holdings of Mexican short-term debt if others did the same, but when others panicked, few remained confident of being repaid. This probably explains why the first international rescue package of U.S.$18 billion was unsuccessful in calming the markets. The rescue package plus the international reserves would barely have covered half of Mexico's financial obligations for 1995. Stopping the collapse of the peso required a package of around U.S.$50 billion, equivalent to the total debt payments coming due in 1995.[36]

Elements of this story have been formalized by Ibarra, who highlights the role of the ratio of Tesobonos to reserves in the post-devaluation speculation against the peso, while Cole and Kehoe model the government's inability to roll over its debt as a self-fulfilling debt crisis.[37] The latter may seem paradoxical since Mexico's government debt fell continuously and substantially in the six years preceding the crisis. Cole and Kehoe's argument rests on the maturity structure of the debt (and not only on its level). Their model identifies a crucial interval of debt for which the government will be willing to service the old debt provided that it can roll it over, but will default if it cannot sell new debt. Outside this interval, debt service is presumably either so low that the government will not want to default even if it fails to sell new debt or so high that it overwhelms the costs of default. When government debt is in the critical interval, which the authors call the crisis zone, multiple equilibria exist, and whether default oc-

36. The final package included $20 billion of loan guarantees from the U.S. government, $17.8 billion of credits from the IMF, $10 billion in short-term loans from central banks via the Bank for International Settlements, and several billion dollars of loans from other governments in North and South America. The IMF loan amounted to over seven times Mexico's IMF quota and was unprecedented in the history of the IMF. The Mexican government declared its intention to reduce government spending by 1.3 percent of GDP and to cut the amount of credit granted by state development banks. A National Accord among workers, business, and government was set up to contain the inflationary pressures arising from the devaluation. The Mexican government also emphasized its commitment to market-oriented reforms and pledged to propose constitutional amendments to open previously restricted areas of the economy to private investment and to increase foreign participation in the domestic banking system. As a source of collateral, the Mexican government agreed to have importers of Mexican oil make payments through an account at the Federal Reserve Bank of New York. For an analysis of the package, see Lustig (1997).

37. Ibarra (1997); Cole and Kehoe (1996).

curs depends on whether the government can roll over its debt. A key feature of the model is that the size of the crisis zone depends on the average length of maturity of government debt. With a very short maturity structure, the interval is large and includes levels of debt that are not high by international standards, as was the case in Mexico before the crisis.[38]

This line of reasoning has interesting implications. First, it suggests that the post-devaluation panic could not have taken place if the devaluation had occurred in the first quarter of 1994 (after the Colosio assassination), when reserves were still close to U.S.$20 billion, Tesobonos were about U.S.$6 billion, and the average maturity of government bonds was 306 days (compared to 206 days in December). Given these figures, the economy was probably still outside the crisis zone, and a devaluation at that time would have looked more like the EMS crises of 1992 than the Mexican debacle of 1994. Second, if multiple equilibria indeed existed, this implies that while the post-devaluation financial panic in December was a possibility, it was not inevitable. A Mexican government default was obviously not in the collective interest of investors. The financial panic that was forcing the government to default was a bad equilibrium that was clearly inferior to what collective rationality dictated. To the extent that the self-fulfilling debt crisis reflected the lack of mechanisms for organizing investors' collective action, the argument suggests that the rescue package had a good chance of succeeding—as it did.

Economic Performance after the Crisis and the Medium-Term Prospects

The argument in this paper can be summarized as follows: the critical problems faced by the Mexican economy in the mid-1990s resulted from the fact that trade liberalization and the opening of the domestic bond and stock markets took place in the midst of a persistent real overvaluation of the peso and a high volatility of capital flows. The combination of trade and exchange rate policies was unsustainable, particularly given the vulnerability generated by massive portfolio capital inflows from 1990 to 1993. In this sense, Mexico's success in attracting capital from abroad contained the seeds of its subsequent failure.

38. On the crisis or vulnerability zone, see also Ffrench-Davis (2000); Ffrench-Davis and Ocampo (in this volume).

The legacy of the crisis will be long lasting. The effects on living standards and income distribution were dramatic: average real wages fell by 20 percent between 1994 and 1996. The devaluation caused a deep crisis in the domestic banking sector, which at the time had net foreign currency liabilities and plenty of bad performing loans, and its bailout will more or less double the domestic public debt.

Despite these adverse consequences, however, the economy emerged from the crisis stronger than it was before in several ways. After the deep recession of 1995—and in contrast to the period following the 1982 debt crisis—the economy recovered a growth rate of about 5 percent per year, and open unemployment fell to about 3 percent. Can the country sustain growth at rates higher than those observed since the early 1980s? A number of factors lend some credibility to such a scenario. First, the international environment is more favorable today than in the aftermath of the 1982 debt crisis, despite increased volatility and contagion effects such as those experienced in the aftermath of the East Asian and Russian financial crises. The United States, Mexico's main trading partner, has experienced the longest peace-time economic expansion in history. Mexico's participation in NAFTA has therefore been a bonus, which is reflected in the fact that among Latin American countries Mexico was one of the least affected by the Brazilian currency crisis. While other countries in the region experienced a recession in 1999, the Mexican economy grew at 3.7 percent, with a continued deceleration of inflation to around 12 percent. Moreover, foreign interest rates have remained low compared to the early 1980s, and in contrast to the earlier crisis, the international rescue package successfully prevented the financial panic from degenerating into a decade-long credit run in the international credit markets. In this context, fiscal and exchange rate policies that ensure the economy is operating at full capacity and with a high real exchange rate have greater chances of success now than in the 1980s.

Second, the crisis itself may have positively altered the long-term macroeconomic outlook. The huge real devaluation of the peso abruptly eliminated the unsustainable combination of trade and exchange rate policies that played a major role in the process that generated the crisis. The macroeconomic impact of export expansion has been enhanced in the context of a more open economy and greater integration with the U.S. economy under NAFTA. A comparison of the performance of Mexico's exports during the 1995 crisis with the 1983 recession illustrates the positive legacy of a more open economy. In 1995, the exchange rate increased by 86 percent. In that year, *maquiladora* (in-bond assembly) exports increased by 30 percent, while nonoil and non-*maquiladora* exports expanded by 37 percent. In 1983, following a 466 percent increase in the exchange rate in 1982, *maquiladora* exports increased by 29 percent while non-*maquiladora* and nonoil exports fell by nearly 6 percent. Contrary to what happened in the period 1988–94, net exports expanded after 1995.[39]

Given its magnitude, the real devaluation of the peso also contributed to a reversal of the factors underlying the profit squeeze in the tradables sector and the fall of the private savings rate. The positive effects on the profitability of the tradables sector must, in turn, have contributed to the observed increase in FDI. These investments now represent nearly 20 percent of total private investment, and between 1996 and 1998 they accounted for around 60 percent of total foreign investment (including portfolio inflows). Consequently, a much lower portion of the current account deficit is now being financed by short-term capital than was the case in the first half of the 1990s, thus making the economy less vulnerable to new domestic or external shocks. Private savings increased substantially in 1995 and continued to increase up to 1997. The increase was probably due not only to the real devaluation, but also to the domestic banking crisis and the associated credit crunch.

As credit constraints become less acute, however, the upward trend of private savings may be reversed. The domestic savings rate declined significantly in 1998, which most probably reflects a fall in private savings. Moreover, the banking crisis is far from resolved, and the bailout of the banking system will impose a large burden on the fiscal accounts in the years to come. With the exception of the banking sector, the economy is more robust than in the early 1990s, but it is too early to tell whether policymakers have learned from the experience of 1990–94. The sources of policy concern associated with capital surges (namely, appreciation, resource misallocation, and financial fragility) are not nearly as serious today as they were in the first half of the 1990s. This is the case, however, simply because the magnitude of capital inflows did not return to their previous levels after Mexico regained access to international capital markets.

Appendix

The model of the goods and financial markets used in the paper has two equations, corresponding to the conditions of goods market (or flow) equilibrium and financial market (or stock) equilibrium. The equation of

39. See Ros (1999) for a full discussion.

the IX curve is a locus of real exchange rate (e) and real interest rate (r) combinations along which desired investment (I) is equal to national savings (S_d) plus foreign savings (S_f):

(1) $$I(r, e) = S_d(L, D^*) + S_f(e, L, D^*),$$

where $Ir < 0$, $Ie > 0$, $S_dL > 0$, $S_dD^* > 0$, $S_fe < 0$, $S_fL > 0$, and $S_fD^* > 0$, and where L is total employment, which positively affects both domestic and foreign savings (in the last case, through its effects on the trade deficit) and D^* is the stock of external liabilities, which positively affects domestic savings on account of wealth effects and positively affects the current account deficit (S_f) on account of the higher interest payments abroad associated with a higher level of D^*. Investment depends positively on the real exchange rate (on account of its positive effects on profitability) and inversely on the real interest rate. Given total employment, this IX locus is one along which the nontraded goods market clears through changes in the real exchange rate.

The equation of the financial market (FM) curve refers to the equality between the risk premium (u) on domestic securities and the interest rate differential between domestic and foreign short-term securities, adjusted for exchange rate expectations. The risk premium is assumed to be a function of an exogenous component (u_o) reflecting investors' subjective perceptions on country risk and the stock of external liabilities (D^*):[40]

(2) $$r = r^* + e^e + u \text{ and } u = u(D^*, u_o),$$

where r^* is the real foreign interest rate. Expected depreciation (e^e) is assumed to depend on both the future short-term equilibrium exchange rate (e_{+1}), which for simplicity is given by the solution of the model, and the long-term equilibrium exchange rate (e^*), which is defined as the value of e consistent with a sustainable current account deficit and full employment:

$$e^e = a(e_{+1} - e) + b(e^* - e),$$

where $0 < a < 1$ and $0 < b < 1$.

Exchange rate expectations are thus subject to two forces that tend to offset each other whenever the short-term and long-term equilibrium exchange rates move in opposite directions. Substituting this mechanism of

40. In principle, the domestically held stock of government securities should also be included. The specification in equation 2 is justified if the risk of default on domestically held securities depends on D^*.

expectations formation into equation 2 and solving for e gives the equation of the FM locus:

$$(3) \quad e = \left[\frac{b}{(a+b)}\right]e^* + \left[\frac{a}{(a+b)}\right]e_{+1} - \left[\frac{1}{(a+b)}\right](r - r^* - u),$$

where $u = u(D^*, u_o)$.

Equation 3 defines a downward sloping line in (e, r) space: a fall in the exchange rate tends to generate expectations of depreciation (for given values of e^* and e_{+1}), and this requires an increase in the domestic interest rate to maintain financial market equilibrium.

References

Alarcón, D., and T. McKinley. 1997. "The Paradox of Narrowing Wage Differentials and Widening Wage Inequality in Mexico." *Development and Change* 28(3): 505–30.

Atkeson, A., and J. V. Ríos-Rull. 1996. "The Balance of Payments and Borrowing Constraints: An Alternative View of the Mexican Crisis." *Journal of International Economics* 41 (November): 331–50.

Branson, W. 1985. "Causes of Appreciation and Volatility of the Dollar." In *The U.S. Dollar: Recent Developments, Outlook and Policy Options,* edited by the Federal Reserve Bank of Kansas City, 33–63.

Calvo, G., and E. Mendoza. 1996. "Mexico's Balance of Payments Crisis: A Chronicle of a Death Foretold." *Journal of International Economics* 41 (November): 235–64.

Cole, H., and T. Kehoe. 1996. "A Self-Fulfilling Model of Mexico's 1994–95 Debt Crisis." *Journal of International Economics* 41 (November): 309–30.

Cragg, M., and M. Epelbaum. 1996. "Why Has Wage Dispersion Grown in Mexico? Is It the Incidence of Reforms or the Growing Demand for Skills?" *Journal of Development Economics* 51(1): 99–116.

Dadush, U., A. Dhareshwar, and R. Johannes. 1994. "Are Private Capital Flows to Developing Countries Sustainable?" Policy Research Working Paper 1397. World Bank.

Dornbusch, R., and A. Werner. 1994. "Mexico: Stabilization, Reform, and No Growth." *BPEA 1:1994,* 253–315.

ECLAC (United Nations Economic Commission for Latin America and the Caribbean). 1995. *Latin America and the Caribbean: Policies to Improve Linkages with the Global Economy.* Santiago.

———. 1998. *América Latina y el Caribe: políticas para mejorar la inserción en la economía mundial,* 2d ed. Santiago: Fondo de Cultura Económica and ECLAC.

Ffrench-Davis, R. 2000. *Reforming the Reforms in Latin America: Macroeconomics, Trade, Finance.* Macmillan.

Flood, R., and P. Garber. 1984. "Collapsing Exchange Rate Regimes: Some Linear Examples." *Journal of International Economics* 17(1/2): 1–14.

Gurría, J. A. 1995. "Capital Flows: The Mexican Case." In *Coping with Capital Surges*, edited by R. Ffrench-Davis and S. Griffith-Jones. Lynne Rienner.

Hanson, G., and A. Harrison. 1995. "Trade, Technology and Wage Inequality in Mexico." Working Paper 5110. Cambridge, Mass.: National Bureau of Economic Research.

Ibarra, C. 1997. "Three Essays on the 1994–95 Mexican Currency Crisis." Ph.D. dissertation, University of Notre Dame.

Krugman, P. 1979. "A Model of Balance of Payments Crisis." *Journal of Money, Credit and Banking* 11(3): 311–25.

Lustig, N. 1997. "The United States to the Rescue: Financial Assistance to Mexico in 1982 and 1995." *CEPAL Review* 61 (April): 41–62.

Lustig, N., and J. Ros. 1998. "Las reformas económicas, las políticas de estabilización y 'el síndrome mexicano.'" *Desarrollo económico* 37(148). January-March: 503–32.

Lustig, N., and M. Székely. 1998. "Economic Trends, Poverty and Inequality in Mexico." Inter-American Development Bank (IDB). Mimeographed.

Obstfeld, M. 1986. "Rational and Self-Fulfilling Balance of Payments Crises." *American Economic Review* 76 (1): 72–81.

———. 1994. "The Logic of Currency Crises." Working Paper. University of California, Center for German and European Studies (January).

Ros, J. 1994a. "La economía mexicana en el largo plazo." Paper prepared for the Congreso Mexicano sobre Prospectiva, Mexico City. Fundación Barros Sierra (September 26–27).

———. 1994b. "Mercados financieros y flujos de capital en México." In *Los capitales externos en las economías latinoamericanas,* edited by J. A. Ocampo. Bogotá: Fedesarrollo and Inter-American Development Bank (IDB).

———. 1995a. "Mercados financieros, flujos de capital y tipo de cambio en México." *Economía mexicana CIDE* 4(1): 5–67. Mexico City: Centro de Investigación y Docencia Económicas (CIDE).

———. 1995b. "Trade Liberalization with Real Appreciation and Slow Growth: Sustainability Issues in Mexico's Trade Policy Reform." In *Manufacturing for Export in the Developing World*, edited by G. Helleiner. Routledge.

———. 1999. "La liberalización de la balanza de pagos en México: efectos en el crecimiento, el empleo y la desigualdad salarial." Mimeographed.

Ros, J., and N. Lustig. 1999. "Trade and Financial Liberalization with Volatile Capital Inflows: Macroeconomic Consequences and Social Impacts in Mexico during the 1990s." Paper prepared for the Conference on Globalization and Social Policy, New York. New School University, Center for Economic Policy Analysis (CEPA) (January 10–12).

Ros, J., and P. Skott. 1998. "Dynamic Effects of Trade Liberalization and Currency Overvaluation under Conditions of Increasing Returns." *The Manchester School* 66(4): 466–89.

Sachs, J., A. Tornell, and A. Velasco. 1995. "The Collapse of the Mexican Peso: What Have We Learned?" Working Paper 5142. Cambridge, Mass.: National Bureau of Economic Research.

———. 1996. "The Mexican Peso Crisis: Sudden Death or Death Foretold?" *Journal of International Economics* 41 (November): 265–84.

Trigueros, I. 1998. "Capital Inflows and Investment Performance: Mexico." In *Capital Flows and Investment Performance*, edited by R. Ffrench-Davis and H. Reisen. Paris: Organization for Economic Cooperation and Development (OECD), Development Center.

STEPHANY GRIFFITH-JONES*

5

An International Financial Architecture for Crisis Prevention

The deep integration of developing countries into the global economy has many positive effects. In particular, capital flows to developing countries have important benefits. These benefits are especially clear in the case of foreign direct investment (FDI), which not only is fairly stable but also brings technological know-how and access to markets. Other external flows also have important positive microeconomic effects, such as lowering the cost of capital for creditworthy firms. At a macroeconomic level, foreign capital flows can complement domestic savings, leading to higher investment and growth.

However, large surges of short-term and potentially reversible capital flows to developing countries can have very negative effects. First, these surges pose complex policy dilemmas for macroeconomic management, as they can initially push key macroeconomic variables, such as exchange rates and prices of assets like property and shares, away from what could be considered their long-term equilibrium.[1] Second, and more important, such flows pose the risk of sharp reversals, which can result in very serious losses of output, investment, and employment, as well as dramatic increases in poverty, particularly if they lead to currency and financial crises. This was clearly illustrated by the impact of the crisis in Asia, which

I thank Ricardo Ffrench-Davis and Jose Antonio Ocampo for insightful suggestions and Jenny Kimmis and Jacques Cailloux for their valuable inputs.
1. Ffrench-Davis and Griffith-Jones (1995).

quickly spread to many other countries, including Brazil. The East Asian countries that were hit by the crisis saw their gross domestic product (GDP) fall by 8 percent, on average, in 1998; Mexico saw its GDP fall by almost 7 percent in 1995. Fortunately, output has tended to recover fairly quickly in most cases. The negative effects of a crisis, however, are not just the significant short-term costs, but also include the long-term negative effect on lower productive investment stemming from increased uncertainty.

Asian-style currency crises—and their extremely high development costs—raise a very serious concern about the net development benefits that developing countries receive from large flows of potentially reversible short-term international capital. While the high costs of reversals of those flows are evident, the benefits are less clear. This contrasts sharply with FDI and trade flows, in which the large developmental benefits clearly outweigh the costs. As a result, volatile short-term capital flows emerge as a potential Achilles' heel for the globalized economy and for the market economy in developing countries. If the international community and national authorities do not learn to manage these flows better, such volatile flows could seriously undermine the tremendous benefits that globalization and free markets can otherwise bring.

Causes of Currency Crises

The causes of currency crises always include domestic causes, which differ from case to case. The East Asian countries, for example, displayed serious problems, including important weaknesses in the regulation of their domestic financial systems. In particular, short-term private debt incurred by both banks and nonfinancial firms had been poorly monitored and regulated. Some mistakes also seem to have been made in the liberalization of the capital accounts, as this was reportedly implemented in ways that encouraged short-term flows. Furthermore, several of the East Asian countries had fixed exchange rate policies that pegged their currencies to the U.S. dollar.

However, an important cause of the East Asian crisis was not significant changes in several macroeconomic fundamentals, but rather a sharp deterioration in confidence throughout the region, which spread through contagion effects. Indeed, the most disturbing element in the East Asian crisis was that it affected countries with long track records of good economic management, countries that had been remarkably successful over extended periods in terms of economic growth, dynamism of their export sectors, low rates of inflation, fiscal surpluses, and high rates of saving.

A crucial causal factor for explaining crises thus relates to the behavior of international capital flows. This aspect is linked to certain imperfections of international capital markets. These imperfections almost always featured in the financial panics of earlier times, but their impact has increased significantly as a result of the speed with which capital markets can react in today's global economy, aided by highly sophisticated information technology. Paradoxically, this impact appears to be strongest for economies that are highly successful or that are perceived to be in the process of becoming so. Such conditions trigger a perverse interaction between euphoria in international capital markets and complacency by governments in recipient countries.

Successful economies offer high returns by way of yields as well as capital gains. If international investors can find ways to enter these economies, or if their entrance is facilitated by capital account liberalization, they tend to rush in, generating a surge of capital inflows that affects key economic variables. Exchange rates become overvalued; the prices of key assets, such as shares or real estate, rise quickly and sharply. Both real income and perceived wealth increase. Banks assume that current trends will continue and therefore tend to relax lending standards, lifting liquidity constraints on firms. The balance of payments deteriorates, often quite rapidly, as both consumption and investment rise. Initially, this is not seen as a problem, since foreign lenders and investors are willing to continue lending and investing. Economic authorities thus delay necessary adjustment, confident that their previous success will continue and that crises happen elsewhere.

Then something changes. The change may be domestic or international, economic or political, important or relatively small. Whatever it is, it triggers a sharp modification in perceptions and leads to a large fall in confidence in the economy among internationally mobile investors, that is, both foreign and national investors who are able to take their liquid assets out. The change of perception tends to be both large and quick. A country that was perceived as a successful economy or a successful reformer—for which no amount of praise was sufficient—is suddenly seen as fragile, risky, and crisis prone. The media, and in particular the specialized financial press, contribute in an important way to creating—or magnifying—rapid changes in perceptions: the media suddenly tend to focus on bad short-term news and to underplay more favorable long-term fundamentals. The rating agencies also tend to play a procyclical role, accentuating changes of perceptions. The change of perception tends to be far larger than the magnitude of the underlying change in macroeconomic fundamentals. Furthermore, any weakness in fundamentals is then discovered and magnified by markets. There can be much overshooting. Exchange rates collapse, and stock markets and property prices also fall sharply.

This pattern helps explain the currency and banking crises in the Southern Cone of Latin America in the early 1980s, as well as the Mexican peso crisis of 1994. It also provides important elements for understanding the 1997 East Asian crisis and the more recent crisis in Brazil. There are significant differences among these crises, of course, and among the crises in the East Asian economies, particularly with regard to domestic causes. However, they demonstrate a common denominator in the boom-bust behavior of short-term lenders and investors, driven not just by real trends, but by dramatic changes in perceptions. The complacency of the economic authorities in recipient countries during the period of boom represents another common feature.

Capital and financial markets are special in that although they generally function well, they are prone to important imperfections.[2] Asymmetric information and adverse selection play an important role in explaining these imperfections, since financial markets are particularly information intensive.[3] Furthermore, financial markets offer strong incentives for herding, as individual short-term investors, lenders, or fund managers try to choose the investment or loan that they think is most likely to be chosen by other investors or lenders. Structures within private financial institutions also cause distortions by giving insufficient influence on decisionmaking to research departments concerned with analysis and risk assessment. Further investigation is required to explore the microeconomics of speculation carried out by different categories of market actors. This could be helpful for designing measures, for example, to be taken by the financial industry itself, aimed at helping to inhibit excessive speculative behavior; this would imply designing new systems of reward and punishment that would help prevent crises.

Another relevant area for understanding the East Asian crisis is the analysis of self-fulfilling attacks, that is, crises that arise without obvious current policy inconsistencies. In such cases, the attitude of speculators and investors is crucial to whether an attack occurs. The existence of self-

2. Griffith-Jones (1998).
3. Stiglitz (1994).

fulfilling attacks and multiple equilibria for exchange rates and other key variables implies that good macroeconomic fundamentals are an important and necessary—but not sufficient—condition for avoiding currency crises. There is, at present, a limited understanding of what triggers self-fulfilling attacks.[4] Market actors tend to give rather different explanations for the recent crises. Policymakers in developing countries therefore face the daunting task of playing to moving goalposts to avoid crises. However, certain conditions of vulnerability can be identified (such as high current account deficits as a proportion of GDP or the ratio of external liabilities like net short-term debt, which can easily be reversed). Further investigation on conditions of vulnerability and the nature of triggering events is clearly required to facilitate the prediction of risk and, above all, to improve the prevention of currency crises.[5]

Lessons for Crisis Prevention

Given the volatility and reversibility of some categories of capital flows, the costs of these flows to countries' development may be higher than their benefits, at least during certain periods of time. Consequently, there is a growing consensus among leading policymakers—in developed as well as developing countries—and market actors that important changes are urgently needed both in the international monetary system as a whole and in the policies of recipient countries. By aiming to avoid costly crises and to manage them better if they do occur, these reforms will help limit the negative effects of volatile capital flows. Care must be taken, however, that the measures adopted contribute to broadening access by all developing countries to capital flows, particularly long-term flows.

Actions that are urgently needed include identifying the possible changes required for achieving these aims; ensuring that new policies are based on an in-depth understanding of how different market actors operate; carefully evaluating the potential economic effects of such changes; and adopting the required measures, including possible institutional developments to facilitate their implementation.

The measures discussed below can be divided into three groups.

—Measures that can be taken within existing institutional arrange-

4. Wyplosz (1998).
5. See Ffrench-Davis and Ocampo (in this volume).

ments. Two important examples are, first, the more expansive monetary policy pursued by the U.S. and European central banks in the second half of 1998 to deter the worsening of financial crises and, second, changes in the capital adequacy requirements for short-term and long-term lending that could be initiated in the context of the expanded Basel Committee on Banking Supervision.

—Measures that require some development, expansion, and adaptation of existing institutions, such as the International Monetary Fund (IMF) or the Regulatory Committees that meet under the aegis of the Bank for International Settlements (BIS). Examples include creating new facilities within the IMF (or adapting existing ones) to cope with capital account–caused currency crises (see below); expanding the Financial Stability Forum or establishing a world financial authority to provide appropriate surveillance and prudential regulation of financial intermediaries, not only in developed and developing countries, but also globally; and filling international regulatory gaps to encompass the national regulation of mutual funds and hedge funds and their international coordination.

—Measures that require more institutional radicalism, in the sense of creating new institutions or drastically adapting existing ones. While this is clearly desirable from the perspective of designing institutions and mechanisms to meet the new needs of a globalized private financial system, it is significantly more difficult to achieve. The key problem is that there is no global government to create the new global institutions that are needed to effectively manage a globalized private financial system, and the political process for national governments to create global institutions will undoubtedly be complex and slow. It seems highly desirable, however, to develop a clear vision of an appropriate new international financial architecture that would allow an orderly global financial market to support the development process and that would avoid developmentally and financially costly crises. Such a vision should inform current debates on a new financial architecture.

This paper focuses on issues of crisis prevention. The measures discussed here emphasize improved information and regulation. They attempt precisely to deal with the international capital market imperfections outlined above, which have played such an important part in causing recurrent currency crises.[6] Because crises are so costly, not only to developing coun-

---

6. For an analysis of better crisis management, see, for example, Griffith-Jones, Ocampo, and Cailloux (1999) (also available at www.ids.ac.uk/ids/global/finance/intfin.html).

tries, but also to the international financial community, utmost priority needs to be given to crisis prevention measures. As in medicine, so in finance: prevention is much kinder, and more efficient, than cure.

The focus of the international community in the aftermath of the Asian crisis was on better information, on the one hand, and strengthening the financial system, on the other. This focus was clearly illustrated by the working groups set up under the G-22, an ad hoc group made up of the Group of Seven (G-7) and developing countries, which looked at three areas: enhancing transparency and the disclosure of information; strengthening financial systems both in national economies and globally; and appropriate burden-sharing in the event of international financial crises.

This section briefly discusses the first two areas and examines some stronger and possibly more effective crisis prevention strategies.

Transparency and Information Disclosure

One of the areas initially defined by the G-7 countries and the IMF as central for future crisis avoidance was enhancing transparency and the disclosure of timely and reliable information, basically on developing countries, and facilitating its dissemination to market actors. A flurry of activity in improving information followed. Some of the key data gaps and deficiencies identified were information on foreign exchange reserves, including undisclosed forward positions; maturity and currency exposures of the public and private sectors; and the health of the financial system, including information on nonperforming loans.

A number of steps have already been taken. The most significant are the publication of public information notices (PINs) by individual countries and the IMF's strengthening of the Special Data Dissemination Standard (SDSS), the information standard that the IMF established in 1996 after the Mexican peso crisis. The PINs are prepared yearly by all countries after their Article IV consultation with the IMF, and countries are encouraged to release them speedily. The IMF has also started a pilot program for voluntary release of Article IV staff reports. The strengthening of the SDSS in the areas of international reserves and external debt has been particularly important. Reports now incorporate full details on reserves and any claims against them (for all countries), a practice that was instituted in April 1999.

In addition to information standards, a number of other standards have been defined by the IMF and the BIS, in collaboration with institutions like the World Bank and the Organization for Economic Cooperation and Development (OECD). The aim is to provide codes of good practice. The IMF will promote the dissemination of these standards by incorporating them as conditions for IMF lending. The standards include creating codes of good practice for fiscal transparency and for monetary and financial policies, improving the quality of banking supervision, and addressing issues such as the functioning of financial systems, bankruptcy, and corporate governance.

Though the implementation of these standards may have very positive effects, such as strengthening financial systems, two rather serious concerns need to be raised. First, is the definition of *desirable standards* a sufficiently participatory process, in which the developing countries that will be asked to implement the standards have had enough input in their definition? Should developing countries just be encouraged to adopt these standards, rather than making their adoption a condition of IMF support? These related concerns can be summarized in the phrase, no standardization without participation. Second, will implementing these standards impose excessive administrative and other burdens on governments in developing countries, while not always generating clear benefits for their economies?

LIMITS OF THIS APPROACH   Improved information, along the lines of the changes described above, will clearly be very valuable and will contribute to better market performance. By itself, however, improved information on developing countries most probably will not avert crises. First, the information available to financial markets will never be perfect, and information asymmetries will always exist. Second, better information alone is not sufficient to ensure that financial markets function well, since the key issue is how market actors process and act on the available information. Phenomena such as euphoria and herding imply that bad news is ignored in periods of boom and magnified in periods of bust, with the reverse being true for good news.[7] Third, better information on developing countries has to be complemented by equally important improvements in information on international financial markets.

With regard to the first point, theoretical analysis and practical experience both clearly show that information will continue to be imperfect and that this may cause or contribute to financial crises. A clear forerunner of much of the literature on imperfect information is Keynes, who

7. See, for example, Griffith-Jones (1998).

stresses "the extreme precariousness of the basis of knowledge on which our estimates of prospective yields have to be made."[8] More recently, Eichengreen rather strongly summarizes the limits of improved information for crises prevention: relying excessively on improved transparency "underestimates the extent to which information asymmetries are intrinsic to financial markets. The advocates of information-related initiatives mislead when they assume the problem away."[9]

Indeed, sophisticated and increasingly informed financial markets continue to be extremely volatile. This is the case even in some of the most developed economies in the world. Serious problems and even crises have occurred in banking systems that had the highest ratings on transparency, as illustrated by the banking crises in Scandinavian countries.

One very important reason for imperfect information is that much of the relevant information to which the market reacts comes only with a lag, and it depends on macroeconomic conditions not entirely known in advance. Increasing information that may be relevant to improving microeconomic market efficiency may do little to reduce macroeconomic volatility.[10]

Another source of problems has to do with the processing of information. As pointed out above, the key issue is that investors (and lenders) are increasingly concerned not with what an investment is really worth to a person who buys it for keeps, but with what its market value will be in a few hours or days. To the extent that this is true, available information on developing countries will be less important than how the average market participant is likely to perceive it.

Microeconomic factors, or how financial firms and banks operate, reinforce such problems. This may be related to both costs and firm organization. The board of a financial institution that is deciding whether to invest or lend to a particular country may not be able (or willing) to take account of the rich information available in the research departments of that same institution.[11] Smaller banks, with small research departments, generally rely even less on their internal expertise, tending instead to follow the decisions of other banks. As a result, changes in the opinions of those investors that are considered to be informed may cause noninformed

8. Keynes (1936, chap.12).

9. Eichengreen (1999, p. 80).

10. Ocampo (1999).

11. A recent survey of banks carried out by the Bank for International Settlements shows that most banks take decisions without considering the information available in research and other departments within their own bank.

investors to overreact, since they rely on the formers' lead to make their decisions.

A key problem in this process is that changes in opinion can occur without any significant change of underlying fundamentals. Basically the same information about a country may be interpreted totally differently at different times, because of factors such as the mood of the markets, events in other economies, and so forth. (This effect occurs particularly when a country's economy is in a vulnerable zone.) A good analogy is that a glass may be deemed either half empty or half full, depending mainly on the mood of the viewer and not so much on how clean and transparent the glass is.

A related issue is that of rating agencies. The important weight of subjective factors in rating agencies' risk analysis, together with the significant volatility that has characterized such subjective opinions in the past, has led to suggestions that these agencies could be regulated and that they could improve their risk evaluations. Moreover, the role of these institutions in sovereign ratings could be eliminated, substituting it with ratings made by the supervisory agencies of the countries in which capital flows originate, according to internationally established parameters. This would imply that rating agencies' activities would be concentrated in the evaluation of private risks.[12]

PROVIDING DEVELOPING COUNTRIES WITH ADDITIONAL INFORMATION ON MARKETS   As pointed out above, providing markets with better information on developing countries has to be complemented by providing developing countries with better information on international financial markets. During the crisis that started in Asia, in particular, policymakers in emerging countries (and specifically central banks) encountered important limitations in the essential information available on the functioning of international capital and banking markets.[13] Authorities require more information both on long-term structural changes in these markets and especially on day-to-day changes in the functioning of global and regional markets—and their key actors.

Just as the IMF has led the process of improving the collection and dissemination of information on emerging market economies, which is particularly useful to markets, a parallel effort needs to be undertaken to gather and provide timely information on market evolution to policymakers in

---

12. Ocampo (1999).
13. Based on interviews and personal experience.

emerging markets. This task should perhaps be led by the BIS and coordinated by the newly created Financial Stability Forum, although inputs from other institutions, such as the IMF and the private sector (perhaps through the Institute of International Finance), would be very valuable. These data requirements relate not just to better statistics on international banks' exposures, but also to better information on the international exposures of investment banks, hedge funds, and other institutional investors, including pension funds and mutual funds.

The growth of financial innovations, such as over-the-counter derivatives, have made financial markets more complex and opaque. This has created difficulties in monitoring patterns of activity in these markets and the distribution of risks in the global financial system. The BIS has responded to this situation by drawing up a framework for the more regular collection of statistics on over-the-counter derivatives markets. Such efforts to improve transparency, particularly in relation to derivatives and highly leveraged institutions (such as hedge funds), are widely welcomed, but far greater frequency is required. Major central banks and the BIS could improve the registration of derivatives and institutions like hedge funds by making it obligatory.[14] In addition, developing countries should participate in the relevant working groups where information needs are discussed and decided, so that their information needs on markets are fully considered. In this sense, proposals by the Financial Stability Forum to improve information on hedge funds and other highly leveraged institutions are positive. Their early implementation, which must include the so-called tax havens where access to information is particularly limited, is crucial.

Given the speed with which markets move, the frequency with which relevant data are produced must be very high (and possibly higher in times of market turbulence, when it becomes particularly crucial), and the information must be disseminated immediately to all countries' central banks. In this regard, the BIS could provide a special additional service in which it would play the role of a clearing house of information. Such an effort would require not only that the BIS disseminate the information it gathers directly from markets, but also that the organization collect and centralize the data that individual central banks maintain on their markets and then use that data to compile an aggregate picture, which is outside the scope of any individual central bank. Working via the Internet, the BIS could standardize information requirements, collect the information, ag-

14. Based on interviews.

gregate it, and disseminate it rapidly to all central banks, as well as to other
relevant institutions.

Regulation within Capital-Receiving Countries

Though this study largely focuses on changes in international financial arrangements, establishing appropriate policies in capital-receiving
countries is clearly also of great importance. Considerable responsibility
for discouraging excessive reversible inflows lies with recipient economies.

Recipient countries have the greatest degree of freedom for policymaking in the period of excessive surges of capital inflows. Countercyclical monetary and fiscal policies are essential for reducing the excessive
growth of domestic absorption or current account deficits or both. The recent experience and literature indicate that a tightening of macroeconomic
policies is particularly desirable when indicators of vulnerability to financial and currency crises start to deteriorate quickly or pass certain thresholds. This includes when current account deficits start to grow rapidly,
when the proportion of easily reversible capital flows in total flows is high
and rising, and, particularly, when liquid external liabilities grow rapidly
and approach the level of or even exceed foreign exchange reserves. High
levels of foreign exchange reserves and limits on the level of short-term external liabilities are thus crucial for currency crisis avoidance.

A countercyclical approach should also be applied to the supervision
and regulation of the financial system, especially the banking system. In
boom times, the supervision and regulation of banks—as well as banks'
own credit decisions—should not simply be based on expectations of a
continued growth scenario among borrowers. Potential downside risks, including a slowdown or reversal of capital and a slowdown of the economy
slows, need to be considered in both credit decisions and supervisory evaluations of loans. The risk that the value of collateral, such as property, may
fall sharply in a possible future crisis also needs to be considered in boom
times. A possible measure for regulators to use when asset prices have generally been rising fast is to limit the value of collateral, for example, to an
average of the past three or five years or to a certain percentage of its value.
This countercyclical approach would moderate booms in domestic bank
lending, which often exacerbate the impact of excessive surges of capital
inflows.

If surges of potentially reversible capital are excessive, it may also be
appropriate for recipient countries to take measures to discourage them

temporarily. Some countries (for example, Chile and Colombia) have implemented measures such as taxes and nonremunerated reserve requirements on flows during a fixed period with this objective. Their aim has been threefold: to change the structure of capital inflows by discouraging short-term and potentially reversible flows; to increase the autonomy of domestic monetary policy; and to curb large overvaluation of the exchange rate.[15] There is growing evidence that such measures to discourage excessive inflows have contributed to a relatively more successful management of capital inflows in countries that have applied them.[16] Chile's measures, in particular, contain two attractive features: they are market-based, rather than quantitative, and they apply to practically all short-term flows, which simplifies administrative procedures and reduces (though does not eliminate) possibilities of evasion. Other domestic measures that can be useful for discouraging excessive short-term borrowing include modifying taxes on companies' external borrowing.

The major international financial institutions now explicitly recognize that while they have some limitations and minor microeconomic disadvantages, market measures taken by recipient governments to discourage excessive short-term capital flows can play a positive role if they are part of a package of policy measures that includes sound macroeconomic fundamentals and a strong, well-regulated domestic financial system.

International Regulatory Measures

Recipient countries clearly carry an important part of the responsibility for discouraging excessive reversible inflows, as well as managing them. However, the large scale of international funds—compared to the small size of developing country markets—leads to the question of whether measures to discourage excessive short-term capital inflows by recipient countries are sufficient for dealing with capital surges and the risk of reversal. Source countries must take complementary action, for three strong reasons. First, not all major recipient countries will be willing to discourage short-term capital inflows, and some may even encourage them. For instance, the tax and regulatory measures implemented in Thailand to encourage the Bangkok International Banking Facility encouraged short-term borrowing. Second, even recipient countries that have deployed a

15. Ffrench Davis and Griffith-Jones (1995).
16. See Ffrench-Davis and Tapia (in this volume).

battery of measures to discourage short-term capital inflows have on occasion found these measures to be insufficient for stemming massive inflows. Third, if major emerging countries experience attacks on their currencies, which result in difficulties in servicing their debt, they will be forced to seek large official funding. This fact creates a clear need for international or source country regulation that will discourage excessive reversible capital inflows during booms. Without it, international private investors and creditors might continue to assume excessive risks, based on the euphoria during booms combined with the knowledge that they will be bailed-out if the situation becomes critical. The latter is the classical moral hazard problem.

The international financial crisis provoked a serious debate on how the surveillance and supervision of the international financial system could be strengthened to help prevent economic crises of this sort from happening again in the future. The key issues for strengthening regulation were, first, to significantly improve coordination and consistency of prudential regulation across financial sectors and countries and, second, to fill important regulatory gaps. The debate partly focused on whether existing arrangements should be extended and improved, or whether new institutions should be created to cope with the increasingly globalized financial system, so as to achieve the necessary improvement of international financial regulation and supervision.

THE FINANCIAL STABILITY FORUM   At the more institutionally radical end of the scale, there have been proposals for the creation of a new international body such as a world financial authority or a board of overseers of major international institutions and markets.[17] Such a body would have wide-ranging powers for overseeing global regulation and supervision. A more moderate approach advocates expanding existing institutional arrangements. Both the Canadian and British governments put forward proposals based on this approach in 1998. In the fall of 1998, Chancellor Gordon Brown and Secretary of State Clare Short of the United Kingdom proposed a standing committee for global financial regulation to coordinate the multilateral surveillance of national financial systems, international capital flows, and global systemic risk. The proposed committee would bring together the World Bank, the IMF, the BIS-based Basel Committee on Banking Supervision, and other regulatory bodies on a monthly basis to develop

17. Eatwell and Taylor (2000).

and implement ways to ensure that international standards for financial regulation and supervision were put in place and properly coordinated.

In October 1998, the G-7 finance ministers and central bank governors asked Hans Tietmeyer, then president of the Deutsche Bundesbank, to develop the British proposal and more generally to consider the cooperation and coordination between the various international regulatory and supervisory bodies and to recommend new arrangements. Tietmeyer's report, which was released in February 1999, outlines areas in which current arrangements should be improved, but states that "sweeping institutional changes are not needed to realize these improvements."[18] Instead, the report proposes that a Financial Stability Forum be convened to regularly discuss issues affecting the global financial system and to identify actions needed to enhance stability. The Forum was formally endorsed by finance ministers and central bank governors from the G-7 countries at their February meeting in Bonn, and it met for the first time in April 1999.

The Financial Stability Forum is currently limited in size to forty-seven members, in order to allow for an effective exchange of views and decision-making. Each G-7 country has three representatives on the Forum, from the finance ministry, the central bank, and the supervisory authority.[19] Australia, Hong Kong, The Netherlands, and Singapore were also included in the Forum as members. G-7 representatives have stated that while the Forum will initially be limited to G-7 countries, they envisage that other national authorities, including from emerging economies, will join the process at some stage. The IMF and the World Bank have two representatives each, as do the Basel Committee on Banking Supervision, the International Organization of Securities Commissions (IOSCO), and the International Association of Insurance Supervisors (IAIS). The Bank for International Settlements (BIS), the Organization for Economic Cooperation and Development (OECD), and the two BIS-based committees (the Committee on the Global Financial System and the Committee on Payment and Settlement Systems) all have one representative on the Forum.

The Forum will be chaired by Andrew Crockett, general manager of the BIS, for the first three years, and it will have a very small secretariat in Basel. The Forum has initially met twice a year, beginning in 1999. One of the key aims of the Forum is to better coordinate the responsibilities of the main national and international authorities and supervisory bodies,

18. Tietmeyer (1999, p. 5).

19. The Group of Seven countries are Canada, France, Germany, Italy, Japan, the United Kingdom, and the United States.

and to pool the information held by these various bodies, in order to improve the functioning of markets and reduce systemic risk. Subsequent to its meeting in Washington on April 14, 1999, the Financial Stability Forum defined three ad hoc working groups, which produced their first reports in April 2000. The objectives of the three groups are as follows:

—To recommend actions for reducing the destabilizing potential of institutions employing a high degree of leverage in the financial markets of developed and developing economies. This group is chaired by Howard Davies, Chairman of the U.K. Financial Services.

—To evaluate measures in borrower and creditor countries that could reduce the volatility of capital flows and the risks to financial systems of excessive short-term external indebtedness. This group is chaired by Mario Draghi of the Italian Treasury. Among developing countries, Chile and Malaysia participate.

—To evaluate the impact on global financial stability of financial offshore centers and to monitor the progress made by such centers in enforcing international prudential standards and complying with cross-border information exchange agreements. An assessment will be made of the additional efforts required to avoid underregulation or inappropriate disclosure in offshore centers contributing to global financial instability. This group is chaired by John Palmer, Superintendent of Financial Institutions of Canada.

The working groups comprise officials of developed and developing market economies, international financial institutions, and supervisory groupings, and they draw on work completed or under way in various public and private forums. It is interesting that senior officials from developing countries have been included and that their expertise is seen as particularly relevant. For example, the group that studies measures to cope with volatility of capital flows includes senior representatives from Chile and Malaysia, two countries that have implemented measures to curb inflows and outflows (Malaysia for both and Chile for inflows).

Setting up the Financial Stability Forum is clearly a positive first step toward increasing the coordination and cooperation of the various bodies whose objective is to improve the way markets function in order to ensure global stability. The question lies, however, in whether the Forum, as it has been proposed, will be representative enough and strong enough to address all the relevant issues.

First, the omission of any developing country authorities during the initial years of the Forum appears to be a major error. It has increasingly been accepted, especially since the Mexican peso crisis and the international financial crisis that started in Asia, that developing countries are important actors in this globalized financial system, and that currency crises in developing countries pose both systemic threats to the international financial system and threats to the development prospects of the developing countries themselves. Systematic and formal representation of developing countries on the Forum would increase the legitimacy of the body and expand its range of expertise and perspectives. Developing countries could easily be included without making the new Forum too large. Representatives (such as central bank authorities or regulators) could be chosen on a regional basis, for example, with one Asian, one Latin American, and one African participant. These representatives could be appointed for a fairly short period (for example, two years) and then rotated. This type of representation by developing countries has been working rather well in other contexts, as in the boards of the Bretton Woods institutions.

The Financial Stability Forum is a very important initiative that may be able to reduce vulnerabilities in the international financial system by promoting coordination and cooperation among G-7 regulators, central banks, and international financial institutions. Incorporating representation from developing countries would add valuable insights to the Forum's work and also increase those countries' commitment to its aims.

Second, doubts have been voiced over the institutional strength of the new Financial Stability Forum. With a small secretariat in Basel, semiannual meetings, and no power of enforcement, will the Forum have the sufficient institutional muscle to deal with the tasks that have been identified? Setting up the Forum represents a significant enhancement of the system of global regulation by agreement and peer pressure that has worked reasonably well in the context of the Basel committees. International cooperation at the BIS has always been based on home country control: sovereignty remains at the level of the nation-state, and agreements are reached through negotiation and then implemented, when necessary, through national legislation or regulation. Countries that are not represented at the Basel Committee have also adopted some of their directives (most notably, the capital adequacy standards). In the medium term, however, and in a world of open financial markets, an international body with the power to make and enforce policy may well be needed.[20] This would point toward a body more akin to some kind of world financial authority,

20. Eatwell (1999).

which would be endowed with executive powers along the lines of the World Trade Organization (WTO).

In the meantime, however, the Financial Stability Forum is a very important step in the right direction. Time will tell whether this body is sufficient for promoting international financial stability and to filling the important gaps in financial regulation that undermine such stability.

FILLING REGULATORY GAPS   There are three categories of flows to emerging markets and their associated institutions that may require additional regulation and supervision, whether internationally coordinated or undertaken by the source country. All three types of flows are currently insufficiently regulated, and their surges, as well as outflows, have played a particularly prominent role in triggering recent currency crisis, apparently because they are reversible. The three categories are short-term bank loans, which were particularly important in the Asian crisis; easily reversible portfolio flows made by institutional investors such as mutual funds, which were especially important in the Mexican peso crisis and also significant in East Asia; and activities by hedge funds and other highly leveraged institutions.

International bank loans are already regulated in industrial countries by the central banks; these national regulations are coordinated by the Basel Committee. Existing regulations did not discourage excessive short-term bank lending to several of the East Asian countries, however. Short-term bank loans and their reversal played a major role in the East Asian crisis. Everyone, including regulators, considered most of these East Asian countries (and particularly countries like the Republic of Korea) as creditworthy until just before the crisis. Current regulatory practice also seems to have been an important factor. For example, for non-OECD countries, loans with a residual maturity of up to one year have a weighting of only 20 percent for capital adequacy purposes, while loans over one year have a weighting of 100 percent. This reflects the fact that it is easier for individual banks to pull out from renewing short-term loans. As a result of this rule, however, short-term lending is more profitable for international banks.

A regulatory bias that encourages short-term lending is thus added to banks' economic preference for lending short-term, especially in situations of perceived increased risk. An overall increase in short-term loans, however, makes countries more vulnerable to currency crises, which paradoxically makes banks more vulnerable, as well, to the risk of nonpayment of short-term loans. International authorities need to rapidly examine whether the capital adequacy weighting differential is too large in favor of short-term loans for non-OECD countries, resulting in excessive incentives for short-term lending.

A narrowing of this differential clearly seems desirable. Soon after the Asian crisis, economic authorities, such as Alan Greenspan, proposed increasing the capital charge for short-term loans.[21] No progress was made in this area for a year, however. Only in 1999 was a consultative document issued, with proposals to address the issue. Actions have not yet been taken, although several recommendations support the changes. The issue thus involves not just the definition of appropriate technical measures for a new architecture, but also the development of mechanisms for speeding up the decisionmaking process, especially when basic agreement exists and institutional mechanisms are in place.

With regard to portfolio flows to emerging markets, there is currently no international framework for taking account of market or credit risks on flows originating in institutional investors such as mutual funds (and more broadly on flows originating in nonbank institutions). This important regulatory gap needs to be filled to protect retail investors in both developed and developing countries from the negative effects of excessively large and potentially volatile portfolio flows.[22]

The East Asian crisis confirmed what was very clear in the Mexican peso crisis. Institutional investors, such as mutual funds, strongly contributed to these currency crises, given the very liquid nature of their investments.[23] Regulation should therefore be introduced to discourage excessive surges of portfolio flows. This could perhaps best be achieved by a variable risk-weighted cash requirement for such institutional investors.[24] These cash requirements would be placed as interest-bearing deposits in commercial banks. Introducing a dynamic risk-weighted cash requirement for mutual funds (and perhaps other institutional investors) is within the mainstream of current regulatory thinking. It would require that standards be provided by relevant regulatory authorities or agreed internationally.

The guidelines for macroeconomic risk, which would determine the cash requirement, should take into account such vulnerability indicators as the ratio of a country's current account deficit to GDP, the level of its

21. Alan Greenspan, *Financial Times*, 28 February 1998.
22. Griffith-Jones (1998).
23. BIS (1998); Griffith-Jones (1998).
24. This proposal was elaborated in a joint study by Jane d'Arista and Stephany Griffith-Jones.

short-term external liabilities net of foreign exchange reserves, the fragility of the banking system, and other relevant country risk factors.[25] The process would require a sophisticated analysis to avoid stigmatizing countries unnecessarily through the use of simplistic criteria. The views of the national central bank and the treasury in the source countries, together with those of the IMF and the BIS, should be helpful in this respect. The securities regulators in source countries would be the most appropriate institutions for implementing such regulations, and their actions could be coordinated internationally by IOSCO.

The fact that the level of required cash reserves would vary with a country's perceived macroeconomic risk would make it relatively more profitable to invest in countries with good fundamentals and relatively less profitable to invest in countries with more problematic macroeconomic or financial sector fundamentals. If a country's fundamentals should deteriorate, investment would decline gradually, which should force an early correction of policy and, in turn, stimulate a resumption of flows. Although a requirement for cash reserves on the assets of mutual funds invested in emerging markets could increase the cost of raising foreign capital for the funds, the increased cost would be compensated by a more stable supply of funds at a more stable cost. Furthermore, this smoothing of flows should discourage the type of massive and sudden reversal of flows that sparked both the Mexican and the Asian crises, making such developmentally costly crises less likely.

Given the dominant role and rapid growth of institutional investors in countries such as the United States, the United Kingdom, and France, the proposal for a risk-weighted cash requirement on mutual funds could be adopted first in those countries, without creating significant competitive disadvantages. Subsequently, IOSCO would need to give urgent priority to harmonizing such measures internationally, so as to prevent mutual funds from channeling their investments through other countries and, especially, offshore centers that did not impose the cash requirements.[26] International guidelines would be formulated through international consultations similar to those employed by the Basel Committee in developing the Core Principles for Effective Banking Supervision. For that purpose, IOSCO could set up a working group consisting of representatives of the national securities regulatory authorities in source countries,

25. See Ffrench-Davis and Ocampo (in this volume).
26. The latter point draws on communication with the U.S. Federal Reserve Board, including a letter from Chairman Alan Greenspan.

together with some representation from developing countries. The new guidelines should take due account of relevant existing regulations, such as the European Commission's Capital Adequacy Directive. The Financial Stability Forum, in which IOSCO participates, could facilitate the implementation and coordination of such prudential guidelines and ensure their consistency with the regulation of other institutions (such as banks) and other potentially volatile flows.

The third category of flows, namely, those associated with hedge funds and other highly leveraged institutions (HLIs), requires urgent study to detect and cover existing monitoring and regulatory gaps. The Financial Stability Forum report on this issue, mentioned above, represents a valuable first step. Further careful analysis—both technical and institutional— is required on how hedge funds and other highly leveraged institutions operate and how they can best be regulated to reduce their impact on magnifying the volatility of capital flows, exchange rates, and stock markets in developing countries and thus minimize the negative effect that this volatility has on development and poverty. There is a growing consensus that HLIs can pose important risks both to direct creditors and, under certain market conditions, to the financial system as a whole.[27] The exact nature of the impact of HLIs on magnifying volatility in developing countries is not yet fully understood. The role of hedge funds in the East Asian crisis, for example, is a matter of debate owing to insufficient information and differences in interpretation. Measures designed specifically to address the impact of hedge funds and other HLIs on magnifying volatility in developing countries have not been given sufficient priority on the regulatory agenda. However, policies for managing the risks posed by HLIs to creditors and the financial system as a whole will also help reduce their negative impact on developing countries.

The problem does not just relate to hedge funds, but also encompasses other highly leveraged activities and institutions, such as proprietary desks of investment banks. HLIs can be defined as having three characteristics: they are subject to little or no regulatory oversight, as a significant proportion operate through offshore centers; they are subject to limited disclosure requirements, and their operations are often very opaque; and they take on significant leverage.

Three sets of responses can be used to address the risks posed by the

---

27. This consensus is reflected, for example, in the Basel Committee's report on banks and HLIs (Basel Committee, 1999).

HLIs. These actions are often presented as alternatives, but it would be better to consider them as complementary. The first response is indirect, attacking the issue through the major counterparties of HLIs (mainly banks and securities houses). One possibility is to promote sounder practices in the way banks and securities houses assess risks when they deal with hedge funds and other HLIs. However, further actions by supervisory authorities also seem desirable. In particular, supervisors should impose higher capital requirements on lending or other exposures of banks to HLIs, to reflect the higher risks involved in such exposures as a result of HLIs opaqueness, high leverage, and lack of regulation. Supervisors may also need to formally or informally prohibit banks from lending to a particular class of risky counterparty. Such measures would not only protect banks, but may also stimulate HLIs to manage risks more responsibly.

A second avenue, which is clearly complementary to the first, is to increase transparency on total exposures to HLIs by all financial institutions. For example, the concept of a credit register for bank loans could be extended along the model of the French *central des risques,* which provides banks access to the aggregate amount of bank lending to each company. Such a register would collect and centralize total exposures (both on and off balance-sheet positions) of different financial intermediaries to single counterparties, such as major hedge funds. Counterparties, supervisors, and central banks in both developed and developing countries could then get information about the total indebtedness of such institutions, which would help them assess the risks involved more precisely. For this purpose, the information would have to be both timely and meaningful, especially to take account of rapid shifts in the positions of HLIs. The register should probably be based at the BIS itself or at the Basel Committee on the Global Financial System (formerly the Euro-currency Standing Committee), which already has experience in gathering similar information.

A third avenue is to directly regulate hedge funds and other highly leveraged institutions. Such direct regulation could take a number of forms, including licensing requirements, minimum capital standards, and minimum standards for risk management and control. In a recent report, the Basel Committee on Banking Supervision argues that such a regulatory regime should focus on the systemic risk that is potentially generated by HLI activities owing to their excessive size and risk taking, which could endanger financial stability.[28] If, as seems probable, HLIs also increase the vola-

---

28. Basel Committee on Banking Supervision (1999).

tility of exchange rates in developing countries, this concern should also be addressed in attempts at their regulation.

The first two forms of dealing with HLIs currently have more support than their direct regulation, even though the latter would deal with the problem more directly. The opposition to such direct regulation is based on practical grounds. For example, it is argued that HLIs could restructure themselves so as to escape any regulatory definition that may be instituted. The most frequent argument against direct regulation of hedge funds is that they would be able to circumvent such regulations, because they either are located offshore or could easily move offshore.

The international community can either ignore this problem by accepting the absurd status quo (and incurring continued high costs from the risk of major instability) or tackle it by raising the issue of extending regulation, including possible regulation of mutual funds, to offshore centers. If global supervision and regulation is genuinely accepted as essential in today's world of globalized financial markets, then there is no justification for so-called no-go areas where such regulations can be evaded or undermined. It is essential that offshore centers comply with international standards with regard to both the provision of information and the global regulation of institutions such as hedge funds. A political initiative in this respect could be both effective and useful if it had the clear backing of the G-7 countries, in particular, and support from developing countries. The technical issues involved in applying provision-of-information standards and regulation to offshore centers require further study so as to facilitate political decisions for action in this sphere.

The recent report by the Financial Stability Forum's working group on HLIs and offshore centers contains positive proposals in this direction.[29] The existence of this working group within the Financial Stability Forum provides the institutional mechanism for urgent action in this field. It is to be hoped that the recently suggested measures will be implemented soon. The focus has thus far been on better regulation of financial intermediaries, which is clearly essential. It is the function of financial intermediation more broadly, however, that really should be regulated, including financial intermediation carried out by nonfinancial firms, such as suppliers (who provide credit) or international companies making direct investment. Unfortunately, such intermediation activities are far more difficult to regulate. An essential first step is acquiring a better empirical understanding of the role

29. Financial Stability Forum (2000).

played by nonfinancial intermediaries in channeling private flows, particularly volatile ones, to developing countries.

More generally, further empirical work is required on several issues, including the recent changes in global credit and capital markets; the criteria used by different categories of market actors, such as banks, mutual funds, hedge funds, and foreign direct investors, for entering and exiting countries; and the incentives behind particular patterns of behavior that contribute to speculative pressures on individual countries and to cross-country contagion. A better understanding of behavioral patterns and outflow trends would help policymakers design measures—to be implemented by individual firms, by segments of the financial industry via self-regulation, by regulators, and by governments (for example, via tax measures)—to discourage market imperfections such as disaster myopia and herding, which contribute to currency crises.

A package of measures is thus needed to make currency crises in emerging markets far less likely and to ensure the efficient operation of the market economy in emerging markets, which should be a basis for sustained development. Avoiding crises seems to require some degree of discouragement or regulation of excessive and potentially unsustainable short-term inflows. Such measures will be most effective if they are applied by both source and recipient countries (although the main responsibility lies with recipient countries), if they avoid discouraging more long-term flows (which, on the contrary, need to be encouraged), if they are simple in design and clearly targeted at unsustainable flows, and, in particular, if they are complemented by good policies in the emerging economies.

Conclusions

The seriousness of currency crises in developing and transition countries is a cause of major concern. No one foresaw the depth of the crisis that started in East Asia, for example, or the speed of contagion. Consequently, a sizeable proportion of the world economy entered recession for a considerable period. This not only eroded impressive gains in poverty reduction in the most affected countries, but also led to major increases in poverty.

Steps need to be taken urgently to prevent future crises and to manage them better if they do occur. Some actions can be implemented either within existing institutional arrangements or with some development, expansion, and adaptation of existing international institutions. These include improving information on international financial markets and filling regulatory gaps, in particular in relation to mutual funds and hedge funds, as well as improving the regulation of bank lending to help prevent excessive surges of capital inflows. It is also important, however, to envision—and start building—a new financial architecture that would meet development needs in the context of the new globalized economy. This includes moving toward the creation of a world financial authority, which would carry out prudential regulation of capital flows consistently across countries and financial sectors. Such a world financial authority could build on existing institutions, especially the new Financial Stability Forum. These measures need to be complemented by measures for crises management.[30]

Though international actions are crucial, individual countries must clearly adopt their own policies for preventing currency crises. Relevant measures include more countercyclical macroeconomic and domestic regulatory policies, the strengthening of domestic financial systems, and more prudent opening of the capital account, accompanied when necessary by market-based measures to discourage excessive surges of capital inflows.

References

Basel Committee on Banking Supervision. 1999. "Sound Practices for Banks' Interactions with Highly Leveraged Institutions." Basel Committee Publications 46. Basel.

BIS (Bank for International Settlements). 1998. *68th Annual Report.* Basel.

Eatwell, J. 1999. "Brown Achieves First Step towards Global Stability." *The Observer* (February 28).

Eatwell, J., and L. Taylor. 2000. *Global Finance at Risk.* New York: The New Press.

Eichengreen, B. 1999. *Toward a New International Financial Architecture: A Practical Post-Asia Agenda.* Washington: Institute for International Economics (IIE)

Financial Stability Forum. 2000. *Report of the Working Group on Highly Leveraged Institutions.* Basel: Bank for International Settlements. See www.fsforum.org/reports/rephli. html.

Ffrench-Davis, R., and S. Griffith-Jones, eds. 1995. *Coping with Capital Surges: The Return of Finance to Latin America.* Lynne Reinner.

Griffith-Jones, S. 1998. *Global Capital Flows.* Macmillan.

———. 2000. "Towards a New Financial Architecture: the Management of Crises." In *Financial Globalization and the Emerging Economies,* edited by J. A. Ocampo and others. Santiago: International Jacques Maritain Institute and United Nations Economic Commission for Latin America and the Caribbean (ECLAC).

30. See Griffith-Jones (2000).

Griffith-Jones, S., J. A. Ocampo, and J. Cailloux. 1999. "Proposals for a New International Financial Architecture, with Special Reference on Needs of Poorer Countries." Institute of Development Studies. Mimeographed.

Keynes, J. M. 1936. *The General Theory of Employment, Interest and Money.* Cambridge University Press.

Ocampo, J. A. 1999. "Reforming the International Financial Architecture: Consensus and Divergence." *Serie Temas de Coyuntura* 1. Santiago: United Nations Economic Commission for Latin America and the Caribbean (ECLAC).

Stiglitz J. 1994. "The Role of the State in Financial Markets." *Proceedings of the World Bank Annual Conference on Development Economics.* Washington: International Bank for Reconstruction and Development (IBRD).

Tietmeyer, H. 1999. *International Cooperation and Coordination in the Area of Financial Market Supervision and Surveillance.* Frankfurt: Deutsche Bundesbank.

Wyplosz, C. 1998. "Globalized Financial Markets and Financial Crises." In *Regulatory and Supervisory Challenges in a New Era of Global Finance,* edited by J. J. Teunissen. The Hague: Forum on Debt and Development (FONDAD).

Contributors

Manuel R. Agosin
Universidad de Chile
  and InterAmerican
  Development Bank

Ricardo Ffrench-Davis
UN Economic Commission
  for Latin America and
  the Caribbean

Stephany Griffith-Jones
Institute of Development
  Studies, University of
  Sussex

José Antonio Ocampo
UN Economic Commission
  for Latin America and
  the Caribbean

Jaime Ros
University of Notre Dame.

Heriberto Tapia
UN Economic Commission
  for Latin America and
  the Caribbean

Index

Argentina: currency board in, 19; effect of Mexican crisis in (*1994–95*), 18–19

Balance of payments: crisis in Mexico (*1974–76*), 110; factors precipitating crisis of, 53; Korean crisis of, 44, 46–47. *See also* Capital account; Current account

Bank for International Settlements (BIS): actions to improve transparency, 151; potential role as information clearing house, 151–52; representation in Financial Stability Forum, 155

Banking system, Chile: crisis in (*1981–86*), 87; prudential supervision of, 22, 87–90; role (*1975–82*), 68–78

Banking system, Korea: interest arbitrage of, 55; lending and debt practices (*1997–98*), 46, 55–57; regulation and government guidance of, 50–52; transformation in, 62

Banking system, Mexico: effect of capital surge on, 126–27, 131; effect of financial crisis on (*1994–95*), 136–37; privatization in (*1991–92*), 110, 126

Banking system, Taiwan: foreign banks in, 51; prudential regulation of, 51–52

Basel Committee: on Banking Supervision, 162; Core Principles for Effective Banking Supervision, 160; on the Global Financial System, 162

Brady agreement, 4, 107–10

Brown, Gordon, 154

Capital account: Chilean policy (*1975–2000*), 21–22; effect of open, 26–27, 33; liberalization in Chile (*1975–82*), 68–78; liberalization of Korean (*1991–93*), 20–21, 39–40, 45–46, 54–56, 60–61; price-based regulation for, 33

Capital Adequacy Directive, 161

Capital flows: associated with highly leveraged institutions, 161; causes, effects, and costs of, 141–45; to developing countries, 141–42; into East Asian economies, 2–3; effect of stability of, 30; lack of controls on surges in, 11–16; needing regulation, 158–64; with open capital account, 33; policy to sustain economic growth with volatile, 33–34; volume, composition, and use of inflows, 5, 31–32. *See also* Foreign direct investment (FDI); Portfolio flows

Capital flows, Chile: composition of (*1980–2000*), 79–82, 92; exemptions from controls on, 23, 89; inflows (*1990–95*), 78–90; inflows (*1970s*), 66–67; net inflows (*1977–2000*), 68–70; post-*1997* outflows from, 91–92, 99; pre-1997 inflows, 67; regulation of flows, 22, 88, 93–95, 101; restrictions on inflows, 68–70

Capital flows, Korea: inflows (*1990s*), 20–21, 41, 44, 55–56, 58, 62; outflows (1990s), 42, 44, 57–59

Capital flows, Mexico: inflows (*1989–94*), 4, 108–11, 114, 125, 127–28; outflows related to monetary policy, 131–37

CEPAL
ECLAC

ECONOMIC COMMISSION FOR LATIN AMERICA AND THE CARIBBEAN

ECLAC is one of five United Nations regional commissions. All Latin American and Caribbean countries are members, as are a number of developed nations in America and Europe with strong historical, cultural, and economic ties to the region. Since its founding in 1948, ECLAC has promoted economic and social development and cooperation between nations through training courses, technical assistance, and policy-oriented research projects. As well as providing general economic analysis, these projects also address the particular problems of individual Latin American and Caribbean countries. In recent years, ECLAC has focused its efforts on the challenges faced by the region in achieving sustained (and environmentally sustainable) growth among pluralist democracies. These democracies face very real demands as they find ways to develop their economies in order to benefit the majority of the population. As a result, ECLAC's main focus has been on helping countries improve economic growth and social equity simultaneously. ECLAC, with headquarters in Santiago, Chile, has two subregional offices in Mexico and in Trinidad and Tobago, together with national offices in Argentina, Brazil, Colombia, Uruguay, and the United States.